BLOG for BUSINESS

Leveraging Content
for Online Marketing
+ Lead Generation

By Erik Wolf

Foreword By Jamie Turner

Edited by Greg Bond
and Amy Dittoe

Zodo Group | Atlanta, GA

Blog For Business by Erik Wolf
Edited by Greg Bond and Amy Dittoe
Design and graphics by Travis Stoneback and Erik Wolf

ISBN 978-0-9860237-4-3
Printed in the United States of America

Also by Erik Wolf

Marketing: Unmasked
*Insider's Tips + Tricks for Success
in Small Business Marketing*

For Isabel, who is just starting to understand what her daddy does for a living,

For Ari, who makes every day an adventure,

And for Michele, who makes all of this possible.

ACKNOWLEDGMENTS

I would like to thank all the people who helped made this book happen. My colleagues Greg Bond and Amy Dittoe did a fantastic job of whipping this book into shape and made an incredible editing team. Thank you both for your hard work, patience and perseverance to make this project the absolute best it could have been.

Thank you to my friend Jamie Turner for being gracious enough to write the foreword. I'm very proud to have you associated with this book.

I also need to extend my deepest appreciation for my crew at Zero-G, the best group this side of anywhere engaging in the enterprise of small business marketing. Thank you not only to Greg and Amy but also Chris Ruby, Michael Shihinski and Nina Spencer for putting up with me — and my strange demands — on a daily basis.

And, of course, thank you to my family: you guys make it all worthwhile.

BLOG FOR BUSINESS

**Leveraging Content for
Online Marketing + Lead Generation**

By Erik Wolf

contents

Foreword
XV

Ch.0
Introduction
1

Ch.1
Why Bloggers Get More Business
5

My Grandpa was a Blogger • How Blogging Fits into Small Business Marketing: The Strategy • The Link Between Blogging and Search Engine Optimization • 3 More Ways your Blog can Help Drive Sales • The Writing Style: Blog Means Never Having to Say You're Sorry • The Key To Success: Be Consistent • Overcoming "Blogger's Block" • TAKE ACTION: How to Get More Business Based on the Advice in this Chapter

Ch.2
How To (Successfully) Build a Website
25

SEO is Grounded in Common Sense • Why You're Wrong if You Don't Care How Your Site Ranks on Google • What is White Hat SEO? • If it Sounds Too Good to be True, it Probably is • Why Isn't My Site Ranked Well on Google? • 5 Steps to DIY Search Engine Optimization Success • Why Your Online Marketing Mix Might Need to Include SEO and SEM • Is AdWords a Good Fit for my Business? • TAKE ACTION: How to Get More Business Based on the Advice in this Chapter

Ch.3
Search Engine Marketing: The Basics
53

SEO is Grounded in Common Sense • Why You're Wrong if You Don't Care How Your Site Ranks on Google • What is White Hat SEO? • If it Sounds Too Good to be True, it Probably is • Why Isn't My Site Ranked Well on Google? • 5 Steps to DIY Search Engine Optimization Success • Why Your Online Marketing Mix Might Need to Include SEO and SEM • Is AdWords a Good Fit for my Business? • TAKE ACTION: How to Get More Business Based on the Advice in this Chapter

FOREWORD

I f you're like most people interested in blogging, you're probably pre-sold on the necessity of having one. After all, plenty of us have heard how blogs can be used to drive traffic to a website. And most of us know that a good blog makes Google, Bing and Yahoo very happy. But very few of us know all the details of how to go about setting up, launching and running a blog.

Good news. Erik Wolf has done a terrific job with the book you're reading now. It's all you'll need to know about blogging – complete with tips, techniques and mini-tutorials.

For starters, Erik dives right in to some great information about how to go about setting up your blog. If you're looking for long-winded gobbledygook about blogging strategy, then this book may not be for you. But if you're looking for good, rubber-meets-the-road tips and techniques, then this book will be everything you need.

Erik also provides some excellent insights into how blogs can be used to drive traffic to your website. Then, he uncovers some of the hidden secrets that successful bloggers use all the time. And finally, he suggests some tools you can use to help keep your blog humming for the long run.

Erik's book is an important one. Why do I say that? Well, let's take a look at the modern consumer. Whether they're buying a B2C product like flowers, books, coffee or wine; or buying a B2B service like accounting, interior design or photography, most of them start their research by doing one thing – Googling it.

For example, let's say you're a person interested in reducing your tax bill this year. What's the first thing you'd do? You'd Google "Tips on Lowering My Tax Bill" in order to find some techniques on how to reduce your tax burden.

Now, if there's a CPA out there who is interested in attracting new clients to their business, they have a few options – they can wait for referrals, they can send out a direct mail piece, or they can write a blog post that attracts eyeballs to their website. (Ideally, the CPA will do all three of these things, but you get my point – in addition to the traditional techniques, writing blog posts is a great way to drive leads to your business. Leads = revenue = success.)

The key point is this: Despite all the changes that have taken place in marketing over the past few decades, consumers still start the buying cycle the same way -- by doing research. 63% of the time, that research starts online. Don't you want to be sure your business is there to greet them when they do their homework?

One final point about Erik's book. If you're like most businesspeople, you're pretty busy worrying about your clients, your employees and a whole slew of other important items. That means you don't have a lot of time to spend reading about setting up, launching and running a blog. That's one more benefit of what Erik has written – you won't find page-after-page of endless details about blogging. Instead, you'll find concise, well-crafted tips and techniques that can help you get going quickly.

In other words, you'll find everything you really need.

Jamie Turner
Co-author of
How to Make Money with Social Media
and *Go Mobile*

INTRODUCTION

An Open Letter to the Readers of This Book

To my readers,

Let's start by facing a difficult reality.

The reason marketing is often overlooked by entrepreneurs and small business owners is that it's difficult and time-consuming. After all, how can anyone expect a business owner — already working 10-12 hours a day — to find a significant amount of time to work on marketing?

If you're looking for a marketing system that will run itself without regular intervention on your part, put this book down now. You won't find any shortcuts or get rich quick schemes here.

What you *will* find in this book is a proven path to marketing success that will allow you to minimize your effort and maximize your investment. This book will show you how to do more with less, and how to successfully incorporate search engine marketing, landing pages, lead generation and more into a winning web strategy.

The ability to successfully leverage an online marketing strategy for sales and lead generation generally requires five key components:

1. Quality Content
2. Outreach
3. Consistency
4. Traffic
5. A Great Website

Great content, created and shared consistently will build traffic over time, though don't expect to see great results until you have built a solid foundation in traffic. The culmination of your efforts will generate a great website that will convert visitors into leads and convert leads into clients.

In the coming pages I am going to outline a strategy that will help you fulfill all five of the requirements above. That strategy, like this book, begins with blogging.

As an entrepreneur who uses blogs to increase revenue for my clients, I have found that the results speak for themselves.

In just 18 months, we saw a home contractor's website traffic jump from about 1,400 visitors per month to nearly 6,000. Online lead generation also increased almost fivefold as a result of weekly blogging. In fact, today they have a single blog post that generates over 1,500 visits from search engines every month. That's right. A single page of content now performs better than most business owners would expect from their entire site.

We've seen a 25-year-old consulting firm double its web traffic in less than a year. They never thought their business would thrive online, but they have come to depend on this new revenue stream.

We have seen flooring contractors that never received a single online lead suddenly draw 2-3 sales opportunities per week, and we have seen CPA firms triple their web traffic in a matter of months.

This book outlines the strategies and tactics we used to make it all happen. To top it off, these strategies are successful for small commoditized companies all the way through large specialized enterprises.

If you follow my blogging advice you *will* see an increase in traffic and qualified leads through your site.

If you follow my web development advice you *will* get the high-performance website you always wanted.

And, if you follow my search engine marketing advice, you *will* be able to grow your business through Google, and you won't ever get suckered by another scam artist.

Happy reading,

Erik Wolf

July, 2012

WHY BLOGGERS GET MORE BUSINESS

This past April, a lot of friends and colleagues sent me an article from USA Today discussing how blogging is being replaced by Facebook and Twitter in business marketing strategies. The article stated a few reasons why businesses may be changing their minds about blogging. Notably, ineffectiveness was *not* one of them.

In the small business marketplace, blog abandonment has always been an issue, primarily because blogging is difficult, time-consuming and requires a lot of regular attention. Those of us who are parents can certainly relate; caring for a blog is the online marketing equivalent of raising a small child. But we don't think of Facebook that way. The small business people we encounter look at Facebook like a college-aged child: fairly low-maintenance, requiring only a few minutes of attention at any given time and something you only need to visit with every once in awhile. So, if you have to choose one, why not choose the easier path?

In the big business marketplace, it seems that blog abandonment has a lot to do with market trends. Translation: it's no longer sexy or trendy to have a blog, so internal marketing folks bet on Facebook and Twitter because it's more likely to impress upper management. To paraphrase my friend Brian Cork, a prominent Atlanta business owner: entrepreneurs push a boulder up a hill, intrapreneurs — or individuals tasked with innovating from within large companies — roll the boulder down the hill, and the corporate guys just try to keep the village safe.

In the USA Today article[1], when asked why his company had stopped blogging in favor of Twitter and Facebook, Bank of America's T.J. Crawford said, "We want to be where our customers are."

It's a pretty silly explanation, especially considering the ways so many of us bank in 2012. Heard of online banking or online bill pay? BoA, more than just about any other traditional business, has a built-in online audience that visits very regularly. So while we don't know the real explanation for why BoA stopped blogging, the reason they cited doesn't make a whole lot of sense.

[1]blog4biz.co/usatoday

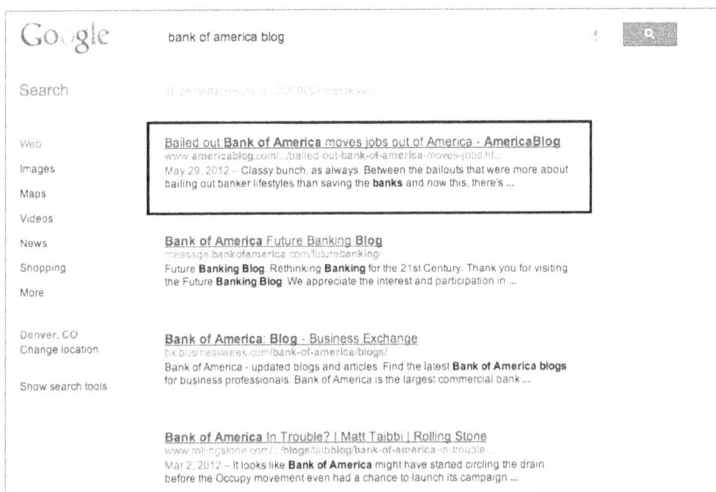

A screenshot of a Google search for "bank of america blog" taken at the time of writing shows that Bank of America no longer controls the #1 spot for that keyword search — another reason why businesses should not be so quick to abandon their blogs

But all this debate is based on the idea that a business is forced to choose between blogging and Facebook, that the two strategies are mutually exclusive. They aren't.

Any strong long-term online marketing strategy (for a non-commodity, non-impulse product or service) is fueled by quality content. The process of blog creation builds discipline by forcing people into a routine. The outcome provides the perfect platform to build a large foundation of content. And once that content exists, it contributes to the effectiveness of all marketing activities including Twitter and Facebook.

For small businesses, blogging provides the key ingredient for integrating your marketing efforts and reducing the time it takes to execute those efforts. Blogging combined with some simple WordPress tricks and free/cheap third party services can drive your marketing with much less effort. It's a process we call *marketing automation.*

Don't spend too much time worrying about what's trendy or what other people are moving towards or away from. Spend your time doing what works. In small business online marketing, blogging remains a big part of a successful strategy.

This chapter will show you how to implement that strategy successfully and leverage your blog to increase sales for your firm.

My Grandpa was a Blogger

Over lunch at a conference in Atlanta this past January, a woman at my table was talking about how uncomfortable she was with all this new technology marketing. She lamented for the "old days" before all this digital media came along.

So I told her about my grandfather.

Back in the 1950's my grandfather was in the jewelry business. He drove around to different towns and talked to people about jewelry: answering questions, telling them what to look for, explaining what the identifying signs of quality were. Once, they even took his picture for a local newspaper; he was helping a young lady try on a beautiful new necklace.

In his own way, 60 years ago, my grandfather was a blogger. He made his living by sharing his expertise and his perspective on issues and questions that were important to his customers. The only difference between what he did and what I do is that he did most of his blogging standing in front of small groups of people. I do most of mine sitting in front of my MacBook.

Blogging and social media technology may still be fairly new, but the hows and whys they work as marketing devices are actually throwbacks to the old days. It's about building relationships, sharing experiences, answering questions and adding value.

Just remember, the new marketing isn't new; you are still striving to engage your audience and leverage your experience to create informative content. If the technology is scary, that's OK, you can always hire someone to push the buttons for you. As long as the content comes from you, you're in great shape to succeed.

How Blogging Fits into Small Business Marketing: The Strategy

A big business marketing effort is usually the advertising equivalent of a "shock and awe" campaign: carefully integrated efforts across multiple media including television, billboards, magazines, web, social and mobile.

But small businesses, constrained by their limits with time and money, are often put in situations where they have to pick and choose what they want to pursue. We eliminate mass media advertising (like television, radio and print) off the bat, because there's almost no way that small businesses can afford enough repetition to get any return on the investment (ROI). So, that leaves word of mouth and online marketing as primary tools. With limited time and money, what can we accomplish online? Do we do Search Engine Optimization (also known as SEO) or social media? Do we start an email newsletter or write an eBook?

A lot of small businesses feel that they only have time and/or money to pursue one of these initiatives at once.

You can pursue it all, and your blog can run the entire machine.

Fundamentally, success in any online marketing initiative is all about content. Yes, there are still SEO consultants who will perpetuate the myth that SEO is based on the proliferation of secret keywords on your website. There are similarly devious "social media experts" who will try to make you believe that success is all about how many followers you have. Both of these claims are 100% false. The only way to find real, sustainable success in either of these initiatives is through the creation and sharing of original, high quality content, and the same goes for just about everything in the online marketing sphere. Writing and posting at least one 300-600 word blog post per week provides you with at least 1,200-2,400 words of quality content per month and 14,400-28,800 words per year. Those are valuable assets that can easily be leveraged for your benefit.

I use the graphic below in presentations to illustrate how blogging directly influences every online marketing initiative a company is likely to have.

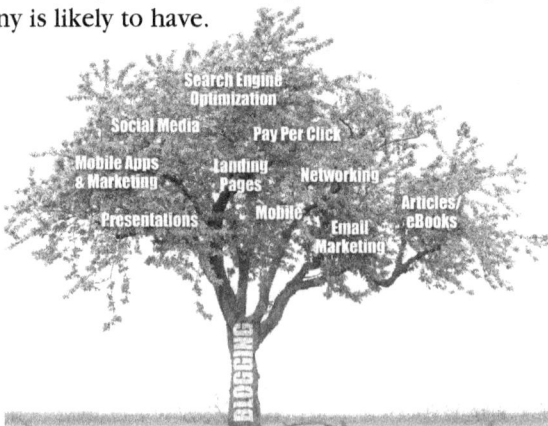

Email Marketing: Most business owners will acknowledge the value of an email newsletter to a marketing plan. Some email marketing services encourage you to use these big, elaborate, magazine style newsletter templates that take forever to write and populate.

A fancy template is completely unnecessary. The more complicated the email, the less likely anyone is to read it. An easy and effective alternative is to use a simple template, lead with a friendly, personalized note about what you and your colleagues are up to, and link to your best two or three blog posts from the month. Now your email is done and, thanks to blogging, it only took you a few minutes.

SEO: By now it should be no secret that Google loves seeing original, relevant content on websites. More than ever before, Google is weighing the frequency of those updates heavily in their algorithm.

That's an advantage, not a liability, for me and other bloggers. Not only does blogging help us build PageRank (Google's measure of trust/importance) but it also ensures that our websites are updated weekly and will grow by 52 pages over the course of a year. As an added bonus, SEO is made a lot simpler thanks to blogging.

Social Media: The really successful people in social media aren't necessarily the ones with the most followers; they're the ones who contribute most to their followers through developing a unique perspective and sharing high quality content. Business owners struggle with what they should talk about or where they should find conversation topics. Blogging gives you a 300-600 word head start every week. Your social media strategy is a no-brainer thanks to blogging.

White Papers, eBooks + Presentations: When you're creating a couple thousand words of content each and every month, you're not just creating blog posts, you're creating building blocks. With some editing, these can easily be used to build other content. The white paper that normally takes three months to write now gets done naturally as part of your weekly blogging effort. The creation of long-form content can be a low-hanging fruit thanks to blogging.

Networking: Whether we're talking about online or in-person networking, the ability to demonstrate value and the ability to follow-up are crucial. Blog posts make wonderful follow-ups and provide great context for anyone looking to do business with you whether as a client, vendor or referral partner. All your follow-ups just got easier thanks to blogging.

Landing Pages and Pay Per Click: You may be wondering how I can possibly tie these efforts into blogging. Easily. Success in AdWords is all about having a relevant offer and the ability to demonstrate value quickly. Blog posts yield eBooks and white papers, and eBooks and white papers are great tools to leverage in landing pages and AdWords campaigns. Google rewards these high quality landing pages by lowering your cost per click. Online advertising campaigns can be more affordable and meaningful thanks to blogging.

Mobile: Business owners frequently ask me about building mobile apps or starting SMS text message campaigns. Executed well, these initiatives can bring tremendous ROI. Like most online marketing, these initiatives require content. By now, I hope it's sunk in that blogging is a great way to create that content.

No, blogging is not a "silver bullet"; you still need to focus on these other initiatives and they will still take time and effort, but they will take significantly less time and effort thanks to blogging. There's no other single initiative that can have the same impact on your strategy as a whole. If marketing can be made much easier by blogging, why not do it all? Blogging makes online marketing success achievable for small businesses in a way that no other investment can.

The Link Between Blogging and Search Engine Optimization

There are many benefits to regular blogging. But did you know that blogging was also the fastest path to good Search Engine Optimization (SEO) and building PageRank[2] with Google? It's a bold, but easily supported claim.

Here's why: the move to add a 300-600 word blog post to your website at least once a week does a lot of the work that just about every SEO expert (including those at Google) highly recommends to help SEO performance. For example a blog provides:

- original, relevant content
- frequent site updates
- an increase in the depth of content in your site over time (blogging once a week for a year adds 52 pages to your website)

[2]blog4biz.co/pagerank

If you're using your blog to drive your social media strategy, there's also a likelihood that your blog is also helping you build backlinks. This is another key aspect to success in SEO.

PageRank is Google's measure of a website's importance/trust on a scale from 0-10. Zero is equivalent to a new site just launched yesterday, and 10 is a site of high importance, like CNN. The difference between each step on the scale is exponential, not linear, which makes each step up harder than the last. It also means, for a variety of reasons, that the vast majority of small businesses will never make it past a 4 or 5, except in extraordinary circumstances.

PageRank factors heavily into Google's algorithm for search. As a result, a site with a PageRank 0 is much harder to rank in SEO campaigns than a site with a higher rank. It basically has no credibility.

Most pages on my website[3] have a PageRank 4, meaning that it's relatively easy for us to improve our rankings for keywords relevant to our business. In fact, in the summer of 2011 we conducted an experiment to increase our visibility for a specific keyword in search results. By blogging and using basic SEO practices, our site increased from #250 to #6 in the search results within two months[4].

Our PageRank 4 at the start of the experiment gave us license to climb in the rankings for relevant keywords. We earned that PageRank by maintaining our blog.

At the start of the experiment, we outlined a straightforward strategy to influence the rankings. We produced a series of targeted blog posts and utilized a few textbook SEO techniques. Both steps are simple enough for just about any business owner to implement without outside help.

Our success in this regard is far from isolated. We've seen similar SEO successes from our blogging clients as well as other clients who engage in regular blogging on their own.

So if you're looking for long-term success in SEO, start blogging and stick with it; you *will* see results.

3 More Ways your Blog can Help Drive Sales

We've already discussed implementing improvements in SEO and to the online marketing environment as a whole, but doubts might persist. You might wonder, *how does regular blogging lead to income?*

I'm going to ignore the remote possibility that your blog will become extremely popular, leading to significant advertising revenues, lucrative book deals and/or a nationwide motivational speaking tour. Instead, I'm going to focus on how a blog can profitably support your core business. Although there are a multitude of possible strategies, we usually like to talk about these three:

[4]As of this writing, about a year after we began this experiment, we still rank #10 for this keyword phrase, though we have not done any proactive work to maintain those rankings in several months.

[3]blog4biz.co/zerog

Use your blog in your sales process

A blog is a great place to document the answers to questions you hear in client meetings. It's also an opportunity to establish yourself as a person who speaks openly, honestly and with authority on issues critical to your clients' success. When a prospect asks you questions or demonstrates an interest in learning more about the pros and cons of a particular type of solution, link an appropriate blog post in your follow-up email after the meeting. It demonstrates expertise and a willingness to share information and will be more effective than any brochure you could have left behind. We believe that good blogging can actually replace traditional collateral for many businesses.

Socialize your best content

Not every post you write will be gold. But when you write something really good, share it with your friends, colleagues and anyone in your contact list that you consider influential or well-connected. These types of messages not only help drive traffic to your post but also create wonderful excuses to stay in touch with people who could potentially refer business (and provide them the ammunition to do so).

Use your blog to make connections

Ever heard of "guilt by association?" There's also status by association. If you can rub elbows with the thought leaders in your industry, your reputation will benefit. Others will seek to do business with you because of your valuable connections. Blogging can help you achieve this.

Visit the blogs and sites of luminaries in your industry and leave poignant comments, linking to related content on your own blog. Send personal emails to these individuals and share your best writing with them. Invite them to guest blog on your site. Your blog can become a very valuable networking tool if you're willing to leverage it.

The Writing Style: Blog Means Never Having to Say You're Sorry

First-time bloggers can have a hard time acclimating to a format that's a little different than most long-form writing. Through every level of school and into our professional careers, we're taught that the things we write should be "complete." We're told that our words should all be carefully chosen, and that our thoughts and arguments should reach logical and definitive conclusions.

Blogging is a little different. The format and writing style is often casual and there are very few actual rules, but, perhaps most importantly, the body of work we're building isn't a single, self-contained post. Instead, our goal is a complex structure that may ultimately contain hundreds of posts connected together like bricks or building blocks.

A single building block isn't a very good toy. There really isn't much you can do with it, and no matter how long you stare at it or how many ways you try to manipulate it you're still not likely to create anything remarkable. Add few more blocks to the mix and the dynamic changes quickly. Suddenly, you can build a variety of things.

Add a hundred more blocks and the possibilities are endless.

The same idea holds true for blogging. The more we obsess about trying to perfect a single post, the longer it takes us to get to the fun part. Once we get over that neurosis and simply start producing content, organic search traffic starts to grow and our social media stream is always current. Soon, the process of creating longer pieces like white papers and eBooks becomes almost as simple as, well, building with blocks.

Don't worry if every post doesn't come out perfectly formed. The nature of blogging is to be a perpetual work in progress where you build on your ideas post by post, where you can always go back and tweak things and where you can flesh out complex thoughts over time.

Never feel that you need to apologize for a post that doesn't meet your high standards, and don't hide material or let it sit on the shelf. If it's not your best work, don't get frustrated and don't let your blog lose momentum. The posts you publish today, the brilliant and the average, are all just blocks in your bucket. You always reserve the right to revisit topics and build on them over time.

The more you publish, the more you learn, the better you get and, most importantly, the more you benefit. So keep building, stop worrying and don't obsess over a less-than-stellar post.

The Key To Success: Be Consistent

Blogging has been around considerably longer than most of the tools we now classify broadly as "social media", but there are still a lot of misconceptions on how to maintain a winning blogging strategy. I've come up with an analogy to help explain the importance of blog maintenance; your blog is a shark.

A healthy shark represents nature's most perfect predator, blending speed, strength, stealth, intelligence and agility with about 3,000 of the sharpest teeth you'll find this side of a Cuisinart. Sharks rule the underwater food chain, and their attack strategies literally stay fresh (they have new teeth coming in every week or so).

Bloggers have similar advantages. A healthy blogging strategy will allow a business owner to create the perfect blend of quality content, web updates, social media, search engine optimization, email marketing and more while expending relatively little effort. And, like sharks' teeth, new blog posts come in every week, creating a steady stream of new marketing weapons.

Sharks have the exact same weakness as blogs; if they stop, they die. Just ask Wikipedia: *many sharks need to remain in perpetual motion to ensure that water passes properly through their gills.* If these sharks stop swimming, they suffocate.

If a blogger stops blogging, their marketing suffocates. Social media efforts become labored. You lose the search engine optimization benefits that come with frequent updates. Your monthly email newsletters devolve into a bi-monthly or quarterly effort.

To keep your marketing machine running smoothly, you need to feed it content constantly. If you plan well, and if you stay disciplined, your marketing will thrive.

The next time you visit someone's website and see that their blog hasn't been updated in weeks or months, remember these two words: dead shark.

A few months ago I chatted with a business owner about

consistency at my favorite coffee shop. He said he wanted to do more marketing, especially online, but has never been able to get into a good rhythm with it.

"My business seems to come in big peaks and valleys," he said. "We go through months when we're really busy and all I have time for is work. Then, we get slow for a little while and I think about doing more marketing."

This is the shark principle in practice. His marketing machine isn't working when he needs it because he lets it die every time he gets busy.

Many small business owners say that they're too busy to do the extra work. They can't keep up with it.

I'm going to challenge that. In my experience, business owners will usually find time for the things that are either A) most important to them, B) tasks they believe they have a strong aptitude for or C) tasks they enjoy most. When marketing doesn't get done on a regular basis, it's usually not because the entrepreneur is too busy; most often it's because marketing is not important/easy/enjoyable enough.

[1]blog4biz.co/uwtb

But if sheer willpower (or "Universal Will To Become[1]" for my fellow Kurt Vonnegut fans) isn't enough to get your marketing done, I have three tips for you:

Make a schedule for yourself

Put recurring appointments on your calendar, set email reminders or implement whatever process makes sense (I make sure that "blog post" shows up in my Teux Deux# every week). If you make your blog a visible priority in your day/week and set deadlines for yourself, you'll find more success than if you just schedule it for "whenever."

Find times to write

If you really can't find an opportunity during busy times to work on marketing, do more when you're slow. Some businesses get swamped during certain portions of the year, and no amount of willpower or scheduling will solve that. Think about what happens to accountants during tax season, for example. We took on a CPA firm in our blogging program earlier this year, and they expressed that exact concern; they said they didn't want to start anything that they couldn't maintain during tax season. We helped solve that problem by doing extra work during the fall, writing material that would not be released until spring. If you give your machine enough fuel at the beginning of a trip, you won't have to fill the tank again for a while.

Consider outside help

I realize this sounds self-serving (the marketing guy suggesting that you hire a consultant to help) but hear me out. If you stopped doing your schoolwork when you were a kid, someone would probably set you right: parents, teachers, etc. If you want to get in shape, but you're lazy about getting to the gym, you might consider hiring a personal trainer. Oftentimes we need other people to hold us accountable. Consistent marketing is no different. Good marketing advisors will do that for their clients, and it can be a difference maker.

Overcoming "Blogger's Block"

There's no question that one of the biggest causes of blogging failure is the dreaded blogger's block. It's the affliction that leaves you sitting in front of a blank computer screen with absolutely nothing meaningful to say. If you're unprepared for it, hitting the wall can sometimes disrupt your blogging cycle. I've said before that at least once a week is a good benchmark for blogging frequency. Missing one post or one week definitely isn't an unforgiveable sin. It happens to everyone.

But if we break the cycle and change our blogging habits, that one week of blogger's block can easily spiral into three weeks, a month or more. Delays will completely disrupt the gains you can reap from a blogging strategy.

So how do we prevent blogger's block from ruining our day and our blog? Here are three tips:

Keep lists

Sometimes, you're really rolling on your blog and the ideas seem to flow out of you like water from a fire hose. That's the perfect time to sit down and make a list of topics that you can use when the great ideas just aren't coming. Keep that list handy (saved on your computer or as a Google Doc that you can access from anywhere) and pop it open the next time you're struggling.

Think about your customers and meetings over the last couple of weeks

The best (and most profitable) blog posts are often the ones that help answer the questions/objections/misconceptions that you encounter in your everyday life as a businessperson. Consider every time you've left a meeting thinking, I wish I could just make them understand why Strategy X was important and how it will work for them. Most business owners experience something like this several times a week. The perfect thing to say comes long after the opportunity you had to say it.

A blog post that offers these after-the-moment insights, summarizes benefits or answers a specific FAQ is solid information and a great sales tool. These are the ideas that should inspire blogs posts.

Do something different.

If writing just isn't happening, try a different medium.

Between our computers, phones and other assorted gadgetry, most of us have several devices capable of recording video and/or audio. A short two-minute monologue about something important makes a great blog post. Talk to your camera about something that's on your mind or an experience you had with a client this week, post it to YouTube or Vimeo and embed the video in your blog or link to it.

If your blog is important to you and part of your overall marketing or business strategy, you have to keep with it even when it's hard. Don't be defeated by blogger's block.

TAKE ACTION: How To Get More Business Based on the Advice in this Chapter

1. Use your blog to share your expertise with a population of potential clients and business partners.

2. Blog consistently, at least one 300 word post a week, every week.

3. Use your content outside your blog: the more you do this, the more likely you are to profit. Use blogging as a basis for email marketing, social media updates, white papers and as a means of following up with prospects and networking connections.

4. Use blogging to support Search Engine Optimization efforts and as support material for AdWords or Search Engine Marketing campaigns.

5. Seriously, do the work! It won't be easy but remember, if you do manage to blog one to three times every week and you do leverage it as I've prescribed above, you will see dramatic changes in traffic within 12 months and you will generate more interest and leads.

HOW TO (SUCCESSFULLY) BUILD A WEBSITE

There is no bigger disappointment than investing heavily in something that backfires or just doesn't pan out. Horror stories of entrepreneurs being ripped off by web developers and online marketing scams are everywhere. Being in the web business myself for well past a decade, I've heard them all.

Some business owners have been burned so badly, they hesitate to invest anything in the web. This is despite the fact that it plays such an important role in small business marketing in our increasingly digital society.

But there's no need to fear. While there may never be a way to ensure overwhelming success in a website design project (according to ZDnet, over 30% of web projects fail[1]) there are many simple ways you can increase your chances of success: making sure that the right things are in the contract, protecting your down payment, choosing the right hosting service and asking the right questions.

Not all web designers and developers are dishonest. Sometimes projects fail for other reasons like mismanaged expectations, poor communications, poor choice in hosting providers or lack of software solutions. Sometimes it's even (gasp!) the client's fault. We've got tips for avoiding all these common failure points in this chapter.

Small business owners can't afford to make major mistakes, so I hope that this chapter saves you from a lot of unnecessary stress if you're not used to managing web people. A little information can go a long way when it comes to protecting you from your own inexperience.

Why this Chapter is Important

Most of this chapter is not strategic marketing advice but rather a lot of "nitty gritty" details about the web development process and you may wonder how or why this fits into a marketing book and why I would devote so much space to it.

Back in the introduction, I told you that there were five key ingredients to success in online marketing. One of those

¹blog4biz.co/zdnet

ingredients was a great website. Unfortunately, if your website never gets off the ground, you can never fulfill the five requirements, all crucial to success.

Following the advice in this chapter will help you ensure that your website is successfully designed, developed and deployed.

Back to Basics

Your website is part of your business, so learn the basics of how websites work. No matter how non-technical you are, understanding website 101 will make you a better shopper for web service providers and less likely to be taken advantage of. Terms you should be familiar with include URL, DNS, IP, Host, Server, SSL, HTML, CSS, FTP, PHP, SQL, mySQL, Linux, .NET, and CMS.

This is the part where business owners typically get that glassy look in their eyes and say that they're not comfortable dealing with this "techie stuff."

That's absolute nonsense and a very poor excuse to stay in your comfort zone. As a business owner, you probably already understand a lot of complex concepts like the difference between your "cash flow" and "income statement" and the differences between an LLC and sole proprietorship. Web development is similar, and it's an important part of your job as the person primarily responsible for your company's marketing. That being said, if you have a marketing person on staff, make them learn this as well.

Don't Hire Just Anyone to Work on your Website

If you've never built a website before, you may not know what to look for in a web developer, designer or agency. First, look at their portfolio and client list (if available). See if their work looks good and functions well, and try to get a feel for what kinds of clients they serve. If you are a small business owner and you see work for much bigger organizations or Fortune 1000 companies, your project may not be a priority for the them. Likewise, if you run a mature small business with 10-20 employees and see that every client on the list is a "solopreneur" startup, they may not be able to handle a business as big as yours.

It's also good to Google your vendors and see what's being said about them online. Check recommendations on LinkedIn and Facebook, and also see what the Better Business Bureau and Web of Trust has to say about them. You might also ask for some client references.

If your vendor comes well recommended and appears to be a good fit, here are some other questions you should ask before moving forward:

Do you follow W3C standards? W3C is the World Wide Web Consortium, the international organization that is charged with setting and maintaining web development standards. Hopefully they will say "yes" or, at worst, "mostly". If they say "no" or "what's the W3C?" that would be a hint to let them go.

Do you build your websites using table or CSS-based layouts? Tables are a primitive way of creating web layouts; it's how those of us that have been in the business for more than 10 years built sites back in the late 1990s and early 2000s. Although tables still have a place in many web layouts, they should not be used to build the framework of the site design. CSS (or Cascading Style Sheets) has been used for that purpose for many years, and it's essential that CSS, not tables, govern your web design. This is primarily for the purposes of updating layouts easily and ensuring that your site is as scalable as possible. Despite best practices, there are still people in this business who have not kept their skills current and have not evolved with their industry to the detriment of their clients.

What programming languages do you know? Advanced knowledge of HTML and CSS is mandatory. Beyond that, your web people should probably have some experience with PHP and javascript for a small business project. The choice of PHP over Microsoft-based languages like .NET is explained later in this chapter.

Do you code from scratch or do you use templates? There really isn't a right or wrong answer here, but you should know what you're buying and what you're paying for. We've seen clients pay thousands for sites that were slightly modified versions of canned templates available for $200 or less. The price you pay should match the level of service provided. You never want to feel like you were shorted after the fact.

What portion of the work do you do yourself and what portion do you outsource? Building websites today requires deeper design skill and deeper programming skill than even just five or six years ago. If a designer outsources part of the project, it isn't necessarily a red flag. But you *should* know which part of the project your vendor really excels in and what you should expect from the process as a whole. You also have the right to know what type of support they receive. Is any of the work is being done overseas? Are they using full-time freelancers or people who moonlight after hours? How much experience does your vendor have working with these people?

Hire Someone Who Makes You Comfortable

Remember, *don't settle*. There are lots of web fish in the sea; if you don't like someone's design work or you feel that their work is dated/clunky/poorly built, hire someone else. It isn't hard to find candidates for a web design project these days, but it can be hard to find a good fit for your needs. Don't rush yourself, and don't hire anyone who gives you a bad feeling.

Buy your Own Domain Name

Make sure you own your domain name; buy it yourself through GoDaddy or a similar service. *Never* allow a developer, designer, consultant, hosting company or other third party to purchase it on your behalf. If someone else purchases a web domain in their name, they own it, not you, and they may or may not be willing to transfer it over to you whenever your relationship ends.

Don't take the chance. Good domain names are difficult to come by, and no one wants to see a company asset that valuable end up in someone else's control.

Remember, you are risking your entire online equity here: your web address, your email address, your search engine rankings, *everything*. Why take such a leap of faith with a third party when you can own it yourself for about $10/year?

A Real-Life Horror Story

I got a call last winter from a former client, Jerry. We had helped Jerry launch his business about three years prior. We developed his logo, website and marketing collateral, and about once a year since that launch, he would hire us to do some minor maintenance work to the site. It was about time for his annual update, so I wasn't surprised to hear from him. But instead of rattling off a handful of web edits, Jerry told me he had come out of a meeting earlier in the day where he needed to show his website to a potential business partner.

The problem? His website wasn't there.

Somehow, Jerry's domain name, his single most important (and most irreplaceable) digital asset, had expired.

When we first worked with Jerry, he had a business consultant, Mike, on retainer. After investigating the situation, I learned that Mike, not Jerry, had originally purchased the domain name. Mike had been renewing the domain every year since, even though he no longer worked for Jerry. But this time, Mike missed the reminder email from GoDaddy and simply forgot to make the payment in time.

Notably, none of this was done with any malicious intent. Mike registered the domain name in the first place because he was trying to help Jerry by saving him an errand. He continued to make the yearly payments because he thought, *It's only a few dollars, why go through the hassle of transferring it?* Mike never intended to harm Jerry's brand or interrupt Jerry's daily business operations. But it happened just the same.

As a result, Jerry would be stuck in limbo for 3-5 business days until the domain would be officially released back into the open market. Then, he would have to purchase it again, hopefully before anyone else did.

I can't stress how important it is for *every* business owner to purchase their own domain name through a reputable registrar like NameCheap (my favorite), GoDaddy or Network Solutions. Almost all domain names cost less than $15/year so there is little financial risk in registering several years at one time, and most registrars will also give you an "auto-renew" option that will automatically charge your card on the renewal date every year.

Never trust your domain name to your consultant, web designer/developer, hosting company, etc. Buy it yourself and make sure it's in your name. If you're not sure your domain is registered in your name, do a WhoIs[2] ("who is") search. If you don't see your name as the registrant, *you don't own it*, and you may suffer the same consequences as Jerry.

Scam Alert: Know who your Domain Registrar is

Assuming that your domain is registered in your name, do you know who your domain registrar is?

I recently received a letter in the mail from an organization

---

[2]blog4biz.co/whois

called The Domain Registry of America, and they had a very official-looking American flag in their logo. And yes, this was the mail mail, not my email. The letter informed me that, as one of my domain names was about 5 months from expiring, I should take immediate action to renew it. If I filled out the information card at the bottom, including my credit card number, they will be happy to renew my domain for me (thereby transferring my URL to their care) for just $30/year.

The letter does not imply that DROA is a government agency, nor do they blatantly misrepresent themselves as anything but a domain registration service that wants your business. But I imagine many people will fill out the form at the bottom of the letter and mail it back simply because it sort of looks like a bill and says in big bold letters at the top right "Domain Name Expiration Notice." After all, if this wasn't a bill, how would they know who I am, what domains I own and when they expire? Unless you have paid extra to make your domain "private" (generally a bad idea for business but not for individuals), your information is completely in the public domain. Doing a WhoIs lookup (the same search I recommended in the previous section about Jerry) on just about any domain name will give you all the details you need to send the owner a Domain Name Expiration Notice of your own.

But I won't be filling out the form. I know where all my domains are registered, and all but a couple reside with NameCheap where my credit card is automagically billed just ahead of the expiration date. I pay about $10/year for each of my domains. The guys that send this snail mail spam are not only playing on people's ignorance, but they're also charging about *three times* the amount of reputable domain registrars. Don't forget where you registered your domain and how to access it. It should be with a proper registrar like NameCheap (*not* your web designer, marketing consultant or hosting company), it should be in *your* name and you should have a username and password that allows you access to your domain controls. And consider signing up for the auto-renewal by credit card. Then you won't even need to open the next *Expiration Notice* you receive from the Domain Registry of America.

All Hosting is not Created Equal

Research your hosting options and learn how to use the online administrator panels. Test drive customer support before buying. If you really want to have some fun, get that friend you have in the IT business to test drive customer support for you and ask the really tough questions. Don't just buy what your web firm offers or whatever is cheapest and most convenient without getting all the information.

If you're a novice, I would recommend using a hosting service that offers cPanel as an administration tool. cPanel is a web-based server management system that is easy to learn and puts a lot of functionality, like the ability to add/edit/delete email and FTP accounts and manage backups, at your fingertips. Plus, it's widely used. The time you spend learning your way around will be transferable to another hosting provider if you ever need to switch. And developers love it.

It's also important that your website is hosted in a real datacenter (with staff, security, appropriate environmental controls, a 24 hour help desk, etc.) and not in your developer's office, basement, garage or bedroom. And please, do not host it yourself or through a friend or family member no matter now technically competent they are.

Make Sure You Have Access: You Never Know when You'll Need it

Make sure that your hosting company, developer or designer provides you with all the necessary passwords and credentials to access your files directly should you ever need to. Note that this is not necessarily an indication of mistrust in your web people, but the unexpected can happen. Should your developer ever move, go on an extended vacation or become sick or hurt, you could have a problem.

The specific items you should have are an FTP login, a login for a web-based hosting administration panel and a login for your content management system, if you have one.

Get Backups, *Lots* of Backups

Ask your web developer for all the files you would need to reproduce your website should you ever need to. Also, make sure you know how to make backups of your site (including any databases) and that this process happens regularly. Unless specifically outlined in a contract or service agreement, backups are likely *not* being done automagically by your developers or your hosting firm. Set a recurring calendar reminder to help you ensure that it gets done.

You Need a CMS and your CMS Should be WordPress

Times have changed. It might have been cost prohibitive for a small business owner to have a content managed website a few years ago, but now every business can and should have one of these tools built into their website. If you have never seen one, a Content Management System (CMS for short) is a password-protected portion of your site where you can login and edit most of your site content, as well as add, delete and hide pages, via a simple interface not unlike Microsoft Word or Google Docs. Having access to a CMS does not necessarily mean that you *have* to make all your own edits, but that you *can* should your developer become unavailable, unresponsive or worse.

I've designed/built/deployed hundreds of websites in my career, and in my opinion, WordPress[3] is the best CMS for about 99% of all small businesses out there. But many business owners still have questions…

- Why WordPress? I talked to a web guy that likes _____ (insert Joomla, Drupal, ExpressionEngine, DotNetNuke, custom-built CMS systems, etc.).
- Isn't WordPress just a glorified blogging platform?
- Can WordPress handle eCommerce?
- What can WordPress really *do*?
- How do I know if WordPress is a fit for my site?

Here are four cases for WordPress that will answer many of the questions my staff and I hear on a near daily basis.

[3]blog4biz.co/wp   [4]blog4biz.co/alexa   [5]blog4biz.co/wpstats

Case 1: WordPress is Well Adopted and User-Friendly

Of the top 1,000,000 websites (as ranked by Alexa[4]) only about 26% use a well adopted content management (CMS) platform. However, according to W3 Techs (and as of this writing), WordPress represents 54% of those sites and more than 16% of the top million[5], making it by far the most popular CMS on the web. Prior to the release of WordPress 3.0 in 2010, WordPress represented less than 8% of the top million and about 27% of the CMS market, but it was still by far the most popular CMS platform.

So why the popularity, and why the growth? Because in addition to being open source (i.e., free) and easy to design and develop for, WordPress is also extremely user-friendly. And trust me, I know; my firm has been developing on WordPress since 2007. We were among the first agencies in the country to adopt WordPress as a full-fledged publishing platform, and we have trained hundreds of new users with an extraordinarily high success rate. A content management system is only as good as the business owner's ability to take advantage of it once the site is live. WordPress accomplishes that goal far beyond the dozens of CMS platforms my team and I have tested.

Case 2: WordPress has an Incredible Support Community

WordPress owns more than half of the CMS market share, and the most recent version has been downloaded more than 60 million times. If you search for "WordPress Web Developer" on Google you will get more than 40 million results .

Why is this important? Because sometimes things don't go according to plan with web projects and sometimes you hire the wrong designer/developer/firm. The better the market share for your web platform, the more likely you are to find a variety of competent resources to work with you. You shouldn't *plan* to have to fire your web firm, but many small businesses do, and it pays to have a contingency plan. On WordPress you are virtually guaranteed to find a suitable replacement for your web vendor if and when that time comes.

Case 3: WordPress is Flexible

A lot of business owners ask me, "Can WordPress do _____?" The question implies that WordPress is a tool, like a drill or a socket wrench. The drill is a better tool than a socket wrench if you're trying to hang a door, and neither of them would be exactly right if you were trying to hang a picture. A better analogy for WordPress would be to call it a toolbox. While it performs a select few functions extraordinarily well on its own, its real usefulness is determined by the quality of the tools you add to it.

So can WordPress do _____?

Unless _____ is creating, editing and managing static content to be stored in pages or posts on a blog or website, with a fresh install WordPress, the answer is usually going to be *no*. But, with plugins, WordPress can easily be made to do a great many things, including:

- eCommerce
- handling lead generation via forms
- Serving as a photo gallery or portfolio
- Serving as a video library
- Managing customer or product information
- Forums

- Wikis
- Customer support
- Real estate listings
- More tasks than I can list here

The beauty of WordPress is its ability to do all of this without compromising ease of use. That's the big reason it leaves Joomla, Drupal and the other big name publishing platforms in the dust, despite the fact that they all had a BIG head start. That doesn't mean that WordPress is a solution for everyone, but my rule of thumb is usually to say that a small business should use WordPress unless there's a compelling reason not to. In three years of developing on WordPress, I could count on one hand the number of clients we met that were not good fits. I could even be missing a finger or two.

Case 4: WordPress isn't Just for Blogging Anymore

Yes, WordPress started in blogging and blogging is still very much in its DNA. But WordPress, especially since the release of version 3.0, has evolved well beyond its basic blog roots. Skeptics often ask if their WordPress websites have to look like blogs, and the answer is a great big without-a-doubt, *no*. Developing on WordPress has not changed my firm's design process one bit; anything that can be done in good old

[6]blog4biz.co/wpdev

39

fashioned HTML and CSS can be seamlessly integrated with WordPress. The uniquely open theme structures in WordPress allow for that.

People who believe otherwise usually gleaned that belief by looking through one or more of the many WordPress theme directories available on the web. The vast majority of stock themes made for WordPress (either for free or for sale) are really designed as blogging (not business) themes. But WordPress really can look like anything you want it to.

If you're firm in your belief that WordPress sites are just for people looking for excuses to blog, I could argue that the more your website makes you feel like blogging, the closer you are to making money from it.

Make Sure You OWN Your Website

As we've discussed earlier, you don't need to own the server your website is hosted on. However, *do* make sure that you own the software, design, code and content that run your website. I'm terribly opposed to "site builders" and other deals offered by service providers including, but not limited to, GoDaddy's Website Tonight, Intuit, Web.com and others. These services charge you a flat monthly fee to use their platform. This allows you to customize one of several preloaded design templates based on your preferences.

If you use one of these services, you're not buying a website, you're renting it. That means that you can't move it to another web hosting company if you want, redesign it substantially if your business changes or the mood strikes, add functionality that doesn't come with the package, etc. without starting from scratch with a whole new site. Your website should be able to grow and evolve with your business and you'll never get that through a "rent-a-site."

"Custom" Doesn't Always Mean "Better"

With few exceptions, small businesses shouldn't build custom CMS platforms in today's environment. As recently as 2008 it would have been prudent to consider otherwise; the most popular CMS platforms like Joomla and Drupal[7] were clunky and difficult to program for and use. WordPress also lacked some key features at that time, especially with regard to managing sites more than 20-25 pages. But today, WordPress meets all the content management requirements that the vast majority of small businesses would have. Why start from scratch? And what happens if you go with the custom solution and need to fire your developer shortly after the site launches? You may be stuck with a custom solution that is never upgraded to accommodate changing technology and that other developers may or may not want (or be able to) work with.

There are a LOT of Browsers Out There

One of the most unique challenges in web development today is the number of web browsers and the very different ways they process websites. Most browsers are largely "standards compliant" in the way they read CSS. This group includes Firefox, Safari, Chrome and Opera, though there are still some interesting differences in how they render websites. Internet Explorer is not standards compliant; it has its own rule book, though versions 8 and 9 are a bit more developer-friendly than its predecessors. Additionally, even on the same browser, a site

---

[7]NOTE: While I have never found any use for Joomla, Drupal is a VERY powerful package with some very advanced features, but it's too complex for a novice to use without regular help from a developer.

may look different on a Mac vs. a PC.

And then, there's the growing popularity of mobile devices like smartphones and tablets to consider.

What does this mean for you? In order for your website to work well on all of these browsers, your developer needs to do a *lot* of work and, in many cases, trade-offs need to be made. Think about your priorities and work with your developer to figure out which browsers and platforms are most important to your business.

You may also want to give special attention to whether or not your site should support Internet Explorer 6. With the release of IE8 in 2009, Microsoft declared IE6 to be "legacy software," meaning that they would no longer support it. Given its severe limitations vs. modern browsers (as well as security concerns), many developers and firms have also abandoned support of IE6, though it is still used by some institutions. If you believe it's important that your site function well in IE6, be sure to discuss that specifically with your developer. If you wait until the end of the project to mention something, your developer may want to charge extra to recode the site to meet what they will likely consider to be new specifications.

Get it in Writing

Make sure you have a written contract or service agreement. This is important for several reasons and protects both parties. First, you want to make sure that there is a clear scope of work defined which ensures that you will get everything you paid for. Second, you need to be sure that you have something in writing that affirms your ownership of the design, code and other intellectual property that is created on your behalf (including source design files.) Ask a lawyer; neglecting to get a written affirmation of this kind may make it difficult for you to sell your business one day.

Most web firms will request via contract the ability to use the work they do for you for self-promotion; this is standard and nothing to be afraid of. Many programmers also like to retain the rights to their code, and this also is not usually something to be alarmed about. The reason coders do this is to help them build a library of useful little programs that they can leverage in other projects to reduce their cost of doing business and save their clients money. Be sure that your agreement protects anything truly proprietary, but otherwise this is fairly benign. And when your developer or agency presents you with a contract, service agreement, or terms and conditions, be sure to read everything carefully before you agree. Don't be afraid to ask questions and request that the answers come in writing.

Protect your Payment

If possible, pay with a credit card. Most developers will request some sort of up-front payment, which is standard operating procedure. If you pay any portion of your project fees up-front with a check and something happens, that money is likely gone forever. If you pay via credit card, however, your credit card company secures your payment and they will get you your money back should your vendor fail to deliver on their obligations to you. Ever heard the story about the business owner who paid 50% up front to his web guy only to have said web guy stop returning his calls after three weeks and ultimately deliver nothing? Don't be that business owner. There is little to fear in making a down payment via credit card, and it affords you considerable security.

Don't Leave any Doors Open

If you sever ties with an employee, vendor or anyone else with access to your website or admin tools, change the login credentials. This is usually easy to do, especially if you are using cPanel to manage your hosting environment and a CMS like WordPress to manage your site.

Your Site, your Responsibility

Try to remind your developers to make a backup of your site before making any changes. Your developer probably knows this is a good idea, but sometimes even the most careful people will cut a corner. Remember that your website is your property, and you, not third party vendors, are ultimately responsible for its care and upkeep. If there are details like this that are important to you, don't be afraid to remind your vendors how you like things done. In doing this, you are not being pushy and you are not being a nuisance; you're just taking proper care of a valuable business asset.

Be a Good Client

I've focused a lot here on the things that you can do to protect yourself from a bad vendor. In many cases, however, it takes two parties to create a less-than-optimal working relationship, so you should also try to protect yourself from, well, yourself. Here are some ways you can do that:

Be Honest: You need to have an open, honest and ongoing dialogue with your web people. Let them know where they stand, what they can be doing better and where they are excelling. Let them know that they need to help manage your expectations as well.

Don't ask for discounts/freebies: Odds are you don't work for free, so it's unfair to expect others to. Pay your web people well, pay them on time, be a good partner and I promise you will get more than your share of favors without even asking.

Be mindful of project scope: When you signed on with your developer, you agreed to a list of deliverables. While a project does tend to evolve between the time it starts and the time it completes, try not to push the envelope too far. If your developer has agreed to build 20 pages of content on your behalf, don't send 40 without discussing how scope will be affected.

Understand your role in the process: Web development is an involved, high-touch process and requires a lot of input from you along the way. You will need to provide feedback and approvals; you may also need to provide written content, images and other assets. Your response time is *critical* to the timing of the project. If at any point you're not sure what is expected of you in the process, get with your developer and make sure you're both on the same page.

Get your web people *full* access to everything they need: Full access would include logins for FTP and web-based administration tools *and* access to your databases. Not doing this will likely result in delays and budget overages. It's also helpful if your server is being supported by someone your developer can lean on. Web developers are not usually qualified as server admins and cannot be expected to troubleshoot the hosting environment.

Test, test, test... And then test some more: Large web agencies have entire departments dedicated to quality assurance testing on the websites they produce. But as it's difficult for writers to edit their own work, it's similarly difficult for a lone developer/freelancer or even a small firm to test their websites objectively. This doesn't mean that they are being careless or neglectful, only that they aren't objective. Seeing your website live for the first time, however, you *can* be objective and so can the other stakeholders in your business, your family and friends.

A partnership is a two way street and the more you treat your web person (or people) like a teammate the more they will appreciate your business and, oftentimes, the harder they will work. If you ever wonder if you're doing all you can to be a good client, just ask; hopefully you'll get some helpful feedback.

It Helps to Cultivate a Morbid Imagination

Always plan for "what if." We all want to think that when we consult a vendor, we are entering into a long and productive relationship and that everything is going to go wonderfully. It's terrific when that happens, but all too often it does not. So when you're about to engage in a web design or development project, be sure to consider all the "What if..." questions:

- What happens if I can't reach you and there's a problem?
- What happens if there's a problem and you can't reach me?
- What happens if we find a bug after launch?
- What happens if, after we launch, we need to part ways? Will other programmers be able to work on the site?
- What if I hire (or fire) an employee? What needs to change?
- What if there's a typo?
- What if someone hacks or vandalizes my site?

- What if the server goes down?
- What if my business model changes? How flexible is the platform we're using?

If you have specific concerns or "What if…" scenarios that are of particular importance to you, make sure that you talk to your developer about them before you engage. You should also take steps to ensure that the answers are documented in writing, preferably within your contract or service agreement with your vendor.

Thinking this way may seem bit morbid or fatalistic, but considering the worst-case scenario ahead of time will not only help you prepare, but may also help prevent it from ever happening.

What Should You Look for in a Web Proposal?

So you want to hire someone to build you a website… fantastic! Unfortunately, even once you have found the most talented/ exciting/dreamy web designer or firm available, you still have to go through the unpleasant rigmarole that takes you from proposal to initial payment. And this is a really crucial part of the project; I've spoken to no less than three business owners in the last week who did not know how to "practice safe site" when they were negotiating their web design agreements and have since run into serious trouble.

So what should you look for and how do you protect yourself? Here are a few tips:

A good web proposal should be *specific*. How many designs will be presented? How many rounds of revision are included? Exactly what other functionality is included in the project? What technologies will the designer or firm be utilizing to create these elements? Even if you don't understand what they tell you about technology, have it documented so you can do some research if need be. Be sure to ask (and have in writing) exactly what web browsers you expect to work with your site.

A good web proposal should be *itemized*. How much of your money is being allocated to each of the elements on your proposal? You should always understand how your money is being spent, and you should also have the ability to line-item veto any features that seem a poor value for the money. Your web designer or firm should give you the information you need to make these types of decisions. Never sign off on an estimate that has only a single lump sum value at the bottom without any other detail on how that number was computed. This is also handy in the event that the project goes awry and you are in the position of having to negotiate a partial refund. Knowing what has not been done, and the dollar value of those items, is very helpful in coming to a quick and fair settlement.

A good web proposal should come with *clear terms*. What exactly is your commitment? When do you start paying? What failsafes exist to protect you, your interests and your investment? Be sure that you and your designer/agency are on the same page about all the implications of starting a web project together; you should share a vision on how to plan for success and what disengagement will look like if things go wrong. These aren't always the happiest or most comfortable conversations, but it's important to be open and honest throughout the process.

How Do You Compare Website Proposals?

As we've discussed, decoding website estimates can be confusing. What can be even more confusing, especially for a less-than-tech-savvy business owner, is comparing multiple proposals and ensuring that they are "apples to apples." They rarely are.

Last fall a potential client received my estimate for building a new company website. They asked me to help sort through all the proposals and explain how they were similar and how they were different.

I was relieved to see that all of the proposals named WordPress as the content management solution. My love of all things WordPress has been well established in this chapter, and my firm has been building websites on top of it since 2007. The similarities ended there, however. None of the other firms on the bid intended to do any original design work. Instead there was an opportunity for the client to select an "off the shelf" theme which they would "customize." But how custom is customized? Does that mean changing a color? An image? How far will the client's site be allowed to evolve from the pre-packaged starting point?

At an entry-level sort of price point, you should expect that the amount of truly custom work would *have* to be limited in order for the design firm to make any money on the deal. What shocked me though was that all of these proposals were *very* expensive for what they were; each was in the neighborhood of $3,000 for what seemed like very little actual work. I've spoken recently to three other entrepreneurs who had spent similar sums (or significantly more) to get half-baked "customized" websites based on similar promises.

The bottom line is that if you are looking for a site that is original, unique and designed specifically to meet predefined business or brand objectives, the odds that you will achieve that by starting with a pre-canned template are very, very slim. And if you've budgeted in the $2-5K range, you should have *many* custom design firms to choose from.

Don't settle for someone else's vague idea of "customized." In choosing the color and upholstery for my car, I might say that it was customized just for me. But aesthetics are just a small part of what business owners are looking for in their websites. It's also very difficult to compare development costs on an apples-to-apples basis because different firms break their costs down differently in estimates. This is why, in the section about what to look for in a web proposal, I suggested you insist on receiving a quote that is detailed and itemized.

If you want a fairly accurate estimate though of what your site *should* cost, there are ways to find it. I developed a very simple calculator to help, and it's available on my website[8].

[8]blog4biz.co/sitecost

TAKE ACTION: How To Get More Business Based on the Advice in this Chapter

1. Hire the right developer/agency. Thirty percent of all web projects fail, and failure in web design often means money and opportunities left on the table.

2. Own all the major assets required to keep your website live including domain name, hosting account, and passwords. Trusting third parties to manage this for you could cause downtime.

3. Have your site built on WordPress.

4. Check for browser compliance.

5. Understand all the terms of your contract with your web firm and that everything that is important to you appears in writing.

SEARCH ENGINE MARKETING: THE BASICS

Search Engine Optimization (SEO) remains a mysterious black box for many business owners. Some think that SEO is all about trickery and black magic, and no one but an expert could ever understand. Some think that SEO is basically just the manipulation of hidden keywords on your website. Both of these assumptions, although commonly held, are pretty far off from reality.

Here are three true statements about SEO that will hopefully provide some insight.

SEO is grounded in common sense.

There is really no magic in SEO; most of it is very simple stuff. When an SEO expert tells you that they are going to "optimize" your site, essentially they are tweaking your web content to make it more useful to Google and the other search engines, especially when it comes to being found for specific keyword phrases. For example, if you wanted to rank well for the phrase "Denver Carpet Cleaning," you would need to have that phrase prominently featured in your content. An SEO consultant will integrate those words into several key areas on your site and into your pages to increase the odds that Google will associate your business with that phrase. If the relevant content is not front and center, it is highly unlikely that Google would ever think that your website was about "Denver Carpet Cleaning."

"Better" websites rank better.

Google's goal as a search engine is to connect its users with the best, most relevant websites available. So what makes a good website? A quantity of good, relevant content that is always current is a big help. Picture two landscapers, one who has a five page website that was launched in 2008 and never touched again and another who has a 50 page website which is updated with new, relevant information several times a month. Which do you think Google will favor? This is the main reason that blogging is said to boost SEO. If you were a landscaper with a five page website and began adding a blog post every week, your site would be 57 pages by the end of the first year. This is all highly relevant, highly searchable content, and your site would *always* be up to date. Site performance is another key; sites that load lightening fast are given preference by Google over slow, lumbering, media-heavy behemoths.

SEO is not black magic.

If someone tells you it is, if they tell you they have the secret sauce to ensure a fast-track to the top of the rankings, *run*. And don't look back. The magic/secret tactics are often considered "black hat" by Google, meaning they violate Google's policies in an attempt to game/trick the system and produce fast results. Why would an SEO company do this? Because they trust that they won't run out of naive business owner prospects looking for an easier road than the other SEO guys promised. The rogue SEO firm also doesn't fear retribution from Google because when black hat tactics are employed, Google punishes the website, not the SEO guy/gal. At the end of the day, it is *your* reputation that gets ruined, not theirs. An SEO firm/consultant should be able to tell you exactly what they are doing on your behalf.

On a related note, it's also important to understand that SEO is not a contest between you and Google. If that were the case, we would all certainly lose. SEO is not a game played against Google but rather a way to work *with* Google. Believe it or not, Google wants you to optimize your website, and they provide their own free guides and forums to help you do that.

Why You're Wrong if You Don't Care How Your Site Ranks on Google

Let's say that I am a respected professional in my field, and I have an established network of quality business connections who provide me most of my business leads by way of referral. I know I need a website; everyone does after all. And while I expect my website to help me establish credibility, I don't need it to help me generate leads. Since I don't count on my site to generate leads, it doesn't matter how easy it is to find me or my business on Google. Right?

Sorry, but it does matter. This argument is built on a major false assumption: that the only people who would search for you are strangers.

But we all know this isn't true; we Google places/businesses/ people we know all the time. We search for our friends and associates, we search for the guy who fixed the air conditioner last year, the pizza place around the corner, that CPA your buddy told you about over lunch and the job candidate we interviewed this morning.

You want your business wants to be found, even if you haven't fully utilized SEO. Regardless of whether Google is part of the lead generation process, it's very often part of the sales process. Accessibility on Google is just as fundamental to establishing online credibility as simply having a website, and perhaps even more so. After all, anyone can have a website and anyone with a little bit of cash in their bank account can have a pretty darn nice one. But it's Google that ultimately decides who's important, who's remarkable and who deserves a place on the much-coveted first page.

This does not mean that every business owner should run out tomorrow and hire an SEO firm. It *does* mean that every business owner should care about how findable their business is.

What is White Hat SEO?

As we've discussed, SEO, or Search Engine Optimization, is the name given to a broad set of tactics said to improve your business ranking on Google and other search engines. It is widely speculated that the SEO expert is the online equivalent of a Jedi master, convincing Google through unseen trickery and manipulation that your website, no matter how unworthy, should be ranked highly on their first page of results. "Yes, Google, these *are* the droids you're looking for." Sound ridiculous? It is.

The myth of the SEO Jedi is centered around the idea that website owners are somehow in competition with Google for their organic rankings. But this is not true. Google *wants* you to optimize your site, and Google *wants* you to rank well. The only catch is that they want you to earn your ranking, and the first path to a better ranking is to build a better website.

I'm not talking in this case about a better looking website. Google is indifferent to aesthetics, though they do care that your site have a good blend of text content, image content and multimedia content. A highly ranked website would have a lot of original, frequently updated/curated content focusing on a fairly narrow set of topics. It would be easy for both search engines and humans to navigate, and it would code cleanly and load quickly. If the site accumulates a lot of inbound links from other websites (also known as backlinks), you should find yourself rewarded handsomely with improved search rankings.

This "build a better website according to Google" strategy is known as White Hat SEO. The supposed SEO Jedi/Ninja/Puppetmaster is often using what the industry calls Black Hat or Gray Hat SEO. Black Hat SEO goes against Google's rules and uses techniques designed to manipulate search results. They may produce some impressive short-term results, but could get your site banned from Google once detected. Gray Hat SEO refers to practices that severely bend Google's rules but tend not to break them.

There's another big difference between White Hat SEO and other practices. While Black Hat techniques work faster, White Hat SEO has more lasting effects and will position you for long term success.

Small business owners probably have a good question at this point: *If I'm going to hire someone to help me with SEO, how can I tell if I'm hiring a White Hat or Black Hat/Gray Hat vendor?*

There are a lot of ways to figure this out, but here are three easy ways to identify a Black Hat SEO practitioner:

If it Sounds Too Good to be True, it Probably is.

There's an old Woody Allen quote that I love: "The wicked at heart probably know something." This is certainly true in SEO. Google and the other search engines are independent companies with a vested interest in protecting the sanctity of their rankings. So how could a third party firm/freelancer possibly guarantee a specific result (ranked number one, ranked on the first page, beat all your competitors) if they were playing by the books? Google decides how websites are ranked, not SEO guys. Run from the ones who make very specific promises of success.

Note that there are some (though relatively few) SEO vendors who work based on "pay for performance" types of programs where the client *only* pays when ranking goals are met. While this arrangement does shield you from the possibility of losing your financial investment, it does not guarantee that white hat tactics are being used to generate those results, nor does pay for performance guarantee that the SEO vendor will guarantee to rank you for terms that will end up being valuable for your business.

The more details, the better.

Ask them *exactly* how they would go about optimizing your site. The White Hat SEO vendor will be very specific about their tactics and will present you with a detailed plan of attack. They have nothing to hide. The Black Hat SEO vendor will likely talk about secret sauces, formulas, tricks, etc. The less they tell you about what they are actually going to do, the more you should be worried.

Consider the source.

Ignore cold emails and cold calls from supposed SEO experts. Reputable SEO providers will be referred by someone you know. We'll cover this in more depth in the next chapter. Remember, SEO (if done properly) is not cheating; it's a legitimate practice designed to make your website better and to incentivize Google to reward you.

Determine the Real-World Value of your SEO Initiative

If you are contracting with someone for your website's SEO, you should understand how SEO is actually impacting your site's business performance. It can be difficult to see through through the fog of SEO strategy and jargon, but you *can* build a bridge from reality to SEO-land by answering two simple questions:

What keywords are driving your traffic?

First and foremost, everyone with a website should have Google Analytics installed on the site. Google Analytics is a 100% free service which is very easy to set up and to use. There are other premium and specialty analytics tools available, but even if you do purchase or use another service, I recommend running Google Analytics as well.

Once your site has generated more than 1,000 visitors, you should have enough data to start picking out trends. When it comes to SEO, the most important trend is seeing what people are "Googling" to find your site. If you log into Google Analytics, type "organic" into the search bar on the left side of the screen and hit enter; these results will automatically show up.

To make the organic search metric even more effective, you should eliminate any keywords that directly reference the name of your company. What you will be left with are keyword phrases that relate to your products or services but don't reference your company directly. These are the searches that allowed to you *directly impact your competition*; each of these visits represents an individual who visited your site *instead* of a competitor's. That's right, good SEO will not only improve your site traffic but will also take clicks away from competitive firms.

This metric will also help demonstrate whether your SEO strategies are effective or not. If the keywords your SEO campaign is targeting aren't among the top results on this screen, you should consider why not. If there isn't an explanation, that is one more piece of the puzzle you need to examine before you blame your SEO person for not doing their job. The next step is to check if there is some other disconnect between your SEO efforts and real world results, like your website.

What is happening to the traffic generated by search results when they arrive at your site?

If you notice that very few of your visitors are clicking through to other pages, SEO failure may not be to blame. There could be any number of reasons visitors aren't sticking around:

- The site might not be engaging enough.
- The marketing campaigns are generating irrelevant visitors (they aren't looking for your stuff, so they leave).

- The site didn't answer their question.
- There wasn't a clear call to action, so they didn't know what to do next.
- They found the answer they were looking for (and were satisfied, but moved on.
- If you are spending all of this time, effort, and money on getting better rankings in search results, you'd better make sure the website isn't dropping the ball.

Why Isn't My Site Ranked Well on Google?

I have a new client who has had a website for well over a decade. In that time Google has indexed nearly 100 pages of content from their site and assigned them a PageRank 4 on their 0-10 scale (an excellent ranking for a small business). So why, they asked, is it so hard to find their site on Google?

Maybe I'm an idealist who puts a little too much faith the the Google meritocracy, but in my opinion, if you are not ranked well on Google, it's probably because you don't deserve to be. We all think we're the best at what we do. We all think our business should be number one on Google. But it's important to remember that Google isn't here to rank the quality of our business or our reputation amongst our peers; they are here to rank the quality of our website and our online influence. Here are three questions to ask yourself in trying to figure out why your search rankings are less than ideal:

Have I made my website Google friendly?

First, try to unlearn the myths and mistruths that you've been told about Search Engine Optimization (SEO) over the years, and ask yourself how much you really know. There's no need to try to become an expert overnight; Google has a really simple, plain-English SEO starter guide that will teach you lot. You should particularly consider the following factors.

I'll cover some of this in more detail in the next section and I would also encourage you to check out Google's excellent starter guide.[1]

- Does site has unique and well-written title and description tags?
- Is your site is easy to navigate?
- Do you have a sitemap.xml file on your server?
- Do you have, whenever possible, more than 300 words of content on every page?
- Do you link between your pages and blog posts?

How well-curated is my site?

How often is it updated? How frequently do you post content? A five-page site you posted in 2007 and never updated is, by just about any standard, much less valuable than a 200 page site that is meticulously curated and updated every week. Yes, that sounds like a lot of work, but consider that a solid blogging strategy will do most of the work for you. A blog post a week creates more than 50 pages a year of original, current, high-quality content.

[1]blog4biz.co/googleseo

Am I pursuing the right keywords?

Let's say I'm the owner of a small software widget consulting firm in Atlanta. It would be difficult to be ranked on the first page of Google for "software widget consulting", because the search is too broad. If that's my goal, I'm competing with *every* widget consulting firm out there. So, it normally helps to narrow your focus; this is what a lot of search marketers refer to as "long tail keywords." Consider refining your keyword terms to include either specific geography (like "Atlanta"), a specialty or, if applicable, both.

For example, a generic term like "wood flooring" would be extraordinarily difficult to secure. However, "Sacramento wood flooring" would be more achievable given that I have now limited my goals to a finite geography. "Sacramento laminate wood flooring" would be even more achievable.

It's easier to be a big fish in a smaller pond than a big fish in a huge ocean. There are a lot of tools out there that can give you insight into the relative popularity of search terms. As with most things, the good ones aren't free.

Another tip: just because it appears that *you* can successfully optimize your site to rank highly for a specific keyword phrase doesn't mean that it's worth the effort. The fastest way, in my opinion, to figure out what keyword phrases are going to be the most profitable for you is to experiment with them using Google's paid search product, AdWords. An AdWords campaign can teach you a lot about your keyword phrases (and the results may surprise you).

Remember, it's no accident or dumb luck that causes firms to win and lose on Google. The winners are working hard every week to improve their websites and help themselves be found.

5 Steps to DIY Search Engine Optimization Success

In an ideal world, we'd all have high-quality white hat SEO people on retainer every month. Unfortunately, the good SEO vendors usually charge $1500-$3000 per month for their services. The good news is that just about any business owner can engage in some level of competent SEO on his or her own. Here are five recommendations that I make to my clients:

Avoid complicated website templates and "software as a service" site-builders.

Any service by which you effectively "rent" the design of your website is a serious no-no. They are bad for your overall website strategy, so they also end up being bad for your SEO initiatives. Many of these services can make content management really burdensome, and Search Engine Optimization is all about content. Build your website in WordPress. Lots of reputable hosting providers like Hostgator and Bluehost also have a very easy one button WordPress install, so novices can do it without help (also see our Increasing Online Success info for more advice on choosing the right platform/vendor).

There are a lot of really helpful WordPress Plugins that can help you streamline your Search Engine Optimization workflow.

I'd recommend installing the following plugins:

- All in One SEO
- Simple Google Sitemap XML
- Jetpack[2]

Also, to reiterate an earlier recommendation, make sure that Google Analytics is running on your site.

Optimize each page for only one keyword phrase, like "Atlanta Online Marketing."

As I mentioned in chapter one, during an experiment last summer, my firm managed to climb from #250 to #6 for a lucrative search term in a matter of weeks. And there was no black magic involved.

Remember that the more specific the term, the less competitive it's likely to be and the greater your chances of success. Also note that the content on the page *must* relate closely with the keyword phrase. If I were to write a blog post about Search Engine Optimization, I should not try to optimize it for keywords relating to branding, email marketing or social media even though those are all part of my business. The keyword phrase you are trying to promote should appear at the front of the Meta Title, at or near the front of the Meta Description, in the page headline, in the first sentence of text and once every 150-250 words or so in the text. Each page or post should also have a hyperlink to another relevant page on the site about once every 100 words. So a 450 word page/post should have about 4 links within the text. Also, each page/post should contain more than 300 words.

Blog

Each post should be at least 300 words and you should blog

---

2 This is not a straight SEO plugin like the others I mentioned, but it does help in two important ways. First, it submits your site updates to search engines in real time. Second, it includes advanced spelling and grammar proofing features, both very important for good SEO.

at least once a week. Search Engine Optimization results will come even quicker if you can blog 2-3 times per week. Here's an easy trick: most people tend to write 600 words or more in a clip. Writing 1000 words at once and then splitting into three posts will generate more Search Engine Optimization value for your time investment. And WordPress allows you to schedule posts in advance, which is a great automation tip for time-strapped folks. Use the same Search Engine Optimization writing guidelines from above.

Sync all your blog posts with social media

Consider Twitter, Facebook, LinkedIn and Google+. If you can muster it, posting on these networks between blog posts is a good idea too. Over time, and especially if the content gets shared within your network, this will help build backlinks to your site which also impacts your SEO.

Why Your Online Marketing Mix Might Need to Include SEO and SEM

A lot of business owners ask me whether they should be looking at SEO or Search Engine Marketing (SEM) to anchor their online marketing strategy. In many cases, the answer might be both.

The thing that's often misunderstood about the SEO vs. SEM discussion is that they work in completely different ways and are used to achieve different ends.

Search Engine Optimization is the equivalent of a workout regimen; it takes a long time to get from "Joe Six Pack" to "Joe, who has a Six Pack". There's no telling how long it will take you to get into really great shape, if you get there at all. Despite compelling email offers to the contrary, there are absolutely no guarantees in SEO. No matter what we do, who we pay or how hard we work, the final decisions as to who gets ranked where rest solely with Google.

And any web marketing strategy that rests on the assumption that Google can be beaten/outsmarted/gamed for more than a few weeks is fatally flawed.

Search Engine Marketing (also known as Google AdWords, Pay-Per-Click, PPC and other known aliases), on the other hand, works like an energy drink or a shot of adrenaline. These are the top results set against a yellow-ish backdrop that you'll see after Googling a set of keywords. SEM gets you to the first page of Google quickly and without a lot of effort. But, like an energy drink, it doesn't last forever. If I've gotten buff in the gym and I stop going for a week, my body isn't going to turn to jelly right away. But three hours after I drink a Red Bull, my "up" is gone. Similarly, once my AdWords budget runs out, so does my tenure at the top of Google's paid search results.

Combining SEO and SEM, however, can produce a balanced campaign approach that yields both short and long-term benefits, a controllable budget and measurable ROI.
SEO/SEM Failure Points

As much as we hope for every search marketing initiative to be a fantastic success, it isn't going to work out that way. In my experience, though, there are three main reasons that these efforts fail, causing clients to lose all — or a substantial portion — of their marketing investment.

The Houdini Effect: What makes a magic trick work? A good magic performance is all about redirection, or distracting the audience for long enough that they miss what's really going on. Unfortunately, much as the vast majority of us are ignorant to the way magic tricks work, many small business owners are ignorant to the workings of SEO.

A lot of SEO vendors use similar redirection tactics in managing their clients. They distract you with vernacular, statistics that usually come without explanation and jokes about how you "probably don't want to know" how optimization works (though many won't tell you even if you ask directly). Similarly, SEM guys will blind you with your ever-improving traffic numbers.

How do you overcome The Houdini Effect? Arm yourself with knowledge. Go to a seminar, offer to buy lunch for an expert you know and pick his/her brain for a while. The real experts are secure enough that they don't have to hide behind anything and will give you honest answers.

Bad Medicine: There's an old Far Side cartoon depicting a student in veterinary school, studying equine medicine. The student was holding an open textbook with a list of common ailments on the left and the associated treatment on the right. The prescribed treatment for *every* horse illness was "Shoot." If we drew the same cartoon about small business websites, the cure for just about every ailment would probably be "More Traffic." Want more leads? You need more traffic! Want to build an email list? You need more traffic! Trying to become a thought leader? You need more traffic! Traffic isn't always the right answer, but it *is* an easy one and, frankly, an answer that a lot of business owners enjoy hearing. Make sure you're working with people who will give you an honest diagnosis of what your site needs.

Toothpicking: You can't walk within 20 feet of a food court without being assaulted with a wide variety of sampler meats on toothpicks. They'll let you try a little bite assuming that you'll learn enough about their food to order a whole plate. This might be a great strategy for lunch, but it's a lousy strategy for SEM. When you "sample" campaigns, whether it's by spending $200 to test AdWords or giving an SEO vendor just one month to produce results, you're unlikely to accomplish anything. In fact, in many cases, you're better off doing nothing at all. I'm not suggesting that small business owners need to go big with their online marketing like an enterprise would. But a lot of business owners who try to toothpick their way into a marketing strategy already have the next step in mind, e.g, *I'll throw $200 at this AdWords campaign to see what happens. If it goes well, I'd spend $3,000 a month.* If you believe in the strategy, spend your time and money accordingly and don't bother toothpicking.

Is AdWords a Good Fit for my Business?

There's something about pay per click (PPC) advertising, and Google AdWords in particular, that intrigues a lot of business owners. I've heard some business folks say that they've benefitted from using AdWords as a means to gain more control over their site traffic. I've heard other people say that advertising on Google is like printing money. This is a myth, by the way; relatively few businesses who try AdWords ever get close to this level.

But as intriguing and seemingly affordable PPC advertising is, a lot of business owners don't know if AdWords is a good fit for them. Here are three reasons it might be and three reasons it might not be.

AdWords might be a good investment if:
You can easily craft a unique, valuable and actionable offer. The real strength of AdWords is not in promoting a set or suite of services or a line of products, but rather very specific products and services. AdWords and PPC are strongest in matching buyers searching for a specific good or service with sellers offering that *exact* thing. If you're concerned that creating a specific offer, or a series of specific offers, for a single product/service in AdWords may compromise your goal of selling *all* your products/services, don't be (see the section coming up in chapter five on why landing pages are important). Remember also that if you are successful in drawing a visitor to your site via AdWords, and if you are successful in converting that anonymous visitor to a lead or, even better, a sale, you have earned the ability to continue marketing to that individual over time.

You want to be on the first page on Google. Everyone does! "Organic" SEO can take months or years and may not work at all. If you want to be on the first page of Google quickly, AdWords is a much safer bet than SEO. Of course, on the flip side of that equation, if you invest in an AdWords campaign for a year and shut it off, all the traffic goes away instantly. However, if you invest in SEO for a year and then fire your SEO guy, your website retains, for a time, the equity it built over that year. But if you're one of those business owners who truly believes that all your website is missing is a little bit of traffic to turn into a lead/sales generating machine, why not try buying that traffic on AdWords for a couple of months before you consider SEO or another long-term type of strategy? That investment will either prove or disprove your theory about traffic, help you refine your keywords before you invest in SEO and give you an opportunity to optimize your online sales process.

You can afford to experiment. Many people want to believe that AdWords is like a factory; money and content go in and sales leads come out. In truth though, PPC advertising is more like a laboratory or test kitchen where you constantly search for the right combination of ingredients to produce the desired outcome. There are companies out there who specialize in doing "AdWords by formula" campaigns for small businesses, but there's no one formula that works for everyone. No matter how successful these campaigns are, know you are leaving money (probably quite a bit) on the table.

AdWords might not be for you if:
You have long, relationship-driven sales cycles. Highly expensive, customized services don't always work on AdWords. This is especially true if the goal is lead generation and not simply branding.

Your budget is less than $500/month. The math usually doesn't work out in your favor when your AdWords budget is low, unfortunately. I have a short video on my website which walks through budgeting in detail[3].

You can't afford to fail. Make no mistake, advertising on AdWords is not for the risk averse. If you do have a reasonable budget, you're probably better off spending on AdWords than any other mass advertising. But you still run the risk of losing

[1]blog4biz.co/sembudget

everything you put in.

AdWords can be a great tool in marketing your business online, but like any form of advertising, it comes with risks. Be sure to do the math (and do it honestly) before embarking on any sort of AdWords campaign. If the numbers don't work out in an Excel spreadsheet before you start your campaign, don't expect to find different results after. After all, when betting on a horse race, very few of us would risk our life savings on the injured horse in the back with the 1000 to 1 odds. Sure, if a miracle happens, we might strike it rich, but common sense would suggest we find a safer investment.

Marketing is no different. It's fine to take risks as long as your risks are calculated, and it's always best to balance risky maneuvers against safer ones. Blogging, for example, is a very safe bet. Do it regularly and your site traffic and lead generation will grow organically. But it takes time. AdWords is a great way to get more business now. But if you're not careful, you might not make back your investment.

TAKE ACTION: How To Get More Business Based on the Advice in this Chapter

1. Stick to common sense and "white hat" approaches exclusively; attempts to trick Google may have dire consequences.

2. Avoid "secret sauce" SEO vendors.

3. Consistently work to improve the quality of your site: its performance, its content, its usability. All of these elements will benefit you in SEO.

4. Use blogging to support all of your marketing outreach

efforts including social media; this factors into Google's formula as well.

5. Consider both SEO (organic search) and SEM (paid search/AdWords) in your strategy. Combining these efforts can help maximize your potential for lead generation.

6. Don't try to dip your toe in the water with a small AdWords campaign hoping that it will be an effective sample for a full blown effort, because you will fail. Budget does play an important part in Search Engine Marketing success.

CHAPTER 4

HIRING THE RIGHT
SEO/SEM HELP

I n the last chapter, I gave an overview of effective small business SEO and SEM practices. But it takes more than knowledge to mount a successful search engine marketing effort; if you're not going to be doing all the work yourself, you need to hire the right firms/individuals for the job.

This chapter is all about what to look for and, in many cases, what *not* to look for in search marketing partners.

If you've read the last chapter, it's fair to say that you know a decent bit about your online presence and the key ingredients for success. Most business owners don't. The truth is that ignorance, myths and misinformation have conspired to create an atmosphere where it's all too easy for SEO/SEM vendors to take advantage of small business people who simply don't know any better.

And in some ways, the search marketing industry has actually been encouraged to conduct themselves in a less than ethical manner. Let's face it, the truth of SEO/SEM is a lot less glamorous than we want to believe. After all, aren't secret ninja tricks, guaranteed results and a supposed inside connection with Google a lot sexier and more intriguing than the reality of hard work and analysis?

Yes, these claims of instant guaranteed success for very little money down are insulting to your intelligence. But the marketplace has taught many vendors that these are the kinds of things that you, the client, actually *want* to hear. And those vendors who play along with the charade are usually rewarded handsomely.

If you read this chapter, however, you'll learn how to avoid the less than savory elements in the search business.

6 Tips for Working With a Vendor

Ask for help in the beginning.

Even if you ultimately intend to manage your search marketing efforts yourself, *do* hire an expert to help you get started. Between the WordPress-based SEO tools I recommended in the last chapter and Google's easy/intuitive tools on the SEM side, there's always the urge to take a DIY approach. Don't waste your time fumbling around trying to learn the ropes; you'll likely waste a lot of time and money before you learn the right way to do everything. Contact someone to help you get started and study their approach. You can always take over management once you learn the tools and the strategy. Consider the fees you pay as tuition in learning AdWords and SEO properly.

Keep everything in your name, not the vendor's.

Make sure that any vendor you work with on an SEM campaign helps you set up your *own* AdWords account. You should have full access, and it should be linked to the vendor's account for management. That way, you maintain control of the account at all times, and you can keep the account if you and your vendor stop working together. Some vendors will put clients under their own account, essentially forcing you to lose your history and campaigns and putting you back at square one if you ever wanted to fire them. Not only will you lose your AdWords configuration, but any reputation you've built with Google will also go away. When you start over, your cost per click will be higher and your ads will not perform like they did before.

Keep tight control of your funds.

You should have the AdWords account linked to your credit card, meaning that you would pay Google directly for the ads as opposed to giving your vendor a budget and asking them to spend it on your behalf. Keep your vendors honest and don't create opportunities that will make it easy for them to steal from you.

Be prepared to make mistakes.

Make sure that your efforts are being managed by real humans, not computer software or proprietary systems. Every campaign is different, and no one has a secret formula that will work for everyone. Be prepared to test, test some more and fail a couple of times along the way before you find your rhythm. Trial and error is the only approach to making a good search campaign whether you're talking about optimization or AdWords. The difference between AdWords experts and normal people is how good someone is at selecting what to trial and how quickly they learn from errors.

Utilize landing pages.

Use and test landing pages for your AdWords and SEM campaigns. There's little point in sending an AdWords prospect to your home page. You are paying Google to help you recruit prospects who are searching for something *specific*. So why send those prospects to your home page, which is usually the busiest and least specific page on your website. For more details on why landing pages work, see Chapter 5 in this book.

A lot of vendors will, by default, just send AdWords or other SEM traffic straight to your home page. Be prepared to challenge them on this. Buying traffic for your home page may add visitors into your online sales funnel, but they are less likely to convert into real prospects.

Stay involved, and hold your vendors accountable.

Take detailed notes on everything your *SEO* vendor does on your behalf, and don't be afraid to do some independent research online to get more information. Don't accept secrets; if your SEO vendor is doing white hat optimization, they shouldn't have anything to hide. Remember, if your SEO vendor does something that goes against Google's rules, *your* site pays the penalty.

True Experts are Never Anonymous

I'll just lay it out: don't hire an SEO or SEM expert that you don't know personally or by reputation through their success with professional acquaintances. If a stranger contacts you by email offering to cure your online search woes, ask yourself this: *If your search engine presence is so awful, how do all these so-called SEO experts keep finding you?* The search guys use Google just like the rest of us, and they contact you through your website because they don't respect your intelligence. Don't hire those people.

The following message appeared in my email recently and I've copied and pasted it here. I haven't edited anything other than removing the company name and contact info:

Hello,

Greetings for the day!

I am "Victoria" and I am contacting you after looking at your website- .

We are a SEO & Web Development Company and one of the very few company which offer organic SEO services with a full range of supporting services such as one way themed text links, blog submissions, directory submissions, article writing and postings, etc.

We are a team of 50+ professionals which includes 18 full time SEO experts. We are proud to inform you that our team handled 100+ SEO projects and obtained 40000+manually built links in the past 1 year.

We will be glad to assist you with offering our services. Please let me know your interest.

Thanks,

Victoria
Online Marketing Consultant

I get 10-12 of these unsolicited offers from people like "Victoria" every single week as do many small business owners. Of course, having worked in this business for my entire adult life, I know the difference between a legitimate expert and someone destined to underwhelm (or worse) with their performance.

When seeking a search marketing expert, talk to people you know. See whom they've worked with and what the relationship was like. And even with a high recommendation from someone you respect, spend some time with a prospective vendor before hiring. A true expert will be willing to spend an hour with you to make sure they can help you; a true expert will help you separate fact from myth and explain how winning campaigns are built; a true expert will tell you not to waste your time or money on an initiative that isn't likely to help you even if they stand to profit from it. And be wary of anyone that appears to be selling a "silver bullet" solution that seems to be the answer to all that ails your online marketing.

This search engine business is complicated stuff, but that's all the more reason to do your homework before you dive in. Talk to people about what you really need. Don't hire a stranger for something this important.

Online marketing experts do not cold call, they do not invade your email and they do not use fake names. When you're talking to a real expert, their *reputation* will precede them, not their spam.

But what's the harm in hiring someone on the cheap to work on your website just to see if it works, regardless of who they are, where the actual work is being done and by whom? This seemingly innocent experiment can have dire consequences for your brand. With online marketing, and search engine marketing in particular, hiring the wrong people can severely damage your online reputation and your credibility with Google and other search engines.

Playing the Pyramid

Consider a line from *The Freshman* (a great movie with Marlon Brando and Matthew Broderick). Broderick's idealistic college student had just accused Brando of being a scam artist. Brando replied, imitating his own character in *The Godfather*, "This is an ugly word, this 'scam.' This is business. If you want to be in business, this is what you do."

It's a funny line and, unfortunately, not terribly far off from reality in a lot of cases. There are many business practices that can be considered unethical, even predatory, without being illegal.

In the previous section, I wrote about the dangers of hiring SEO/SEM people you've never heard of. But there's also a major pitfall in hiring from a group of people you do know. You know them because you've bought cosmetics, legal services, kitchen accessories, plane tickets and maybe even your home gas service from them. That's right, they're Multi-Level Marketers (MLMs)[1], and believe it or not there are several MLM groups selling Search Engine Marketing services.

I will take the high road here and refrain from mentioning these companies specifically by name, but one of the more prominent ones almost rhymes with "BadMove."[2]

I would never hire one of these firms.

First of all, if you don't know how MLMs work, do some research on Mary Kay[3], often held up as the gold standard for these types of businesses. I don't want this section to be interpreted as an indictment of MLMs in general; my main concern is how this model has been applied to SEM services.

Selling cosmetics or home goods is one thing, but in selling ongoing business services, there is a fundamental problem with MLMs. The person selling the service has little business interest in what's good for his or her clients long term. The system doesn't reward salespeople for that. The salesperson has a much greater interest in meeting a quota as quickly as possible and moving on to more profitable activities like recruiting people to work underneath them. I always take umbrage when the person selling me a service has little to gain from my success in using his or her product.

And because just about anyone with a pulse and a willingness to sell a complex service they don't understand can represent these companies, buying from an MLM also means that you likely won't have any direct contact with an expert. Note also that some of these services do not actually drive traffic to *your* site with their ads, they drive traffic to a custom page that they create on *their* site. Visitors are still another click away before they get to experience your brand directly.

[1]blog4biz.co/mlm

[2]blog4biz.co/badmove

[3]blog4biz.co/marykay

No, it's not a scam; it's business. But it's a business that will undoubtedly waste your time and money.

The Mystery Behind Google's Resellers

Who doesn't love a good mystery? Here's one I'd like to read: the mystery of how a small, local business can leverage Google to compete with national behemoths who have much larger marketing budgets. The discomfort small business owners feel in beginning a search marketing campaign stems from four primary questions, and none of them comes with a 100% correct answer:

Whom can I trust?

This is a tough question, though I've tried to answer it in this chapter.

Where do I spend the money?

Part of the problem with search engine marketing, and online marketing in general, is the wide variety of options the Internet offers. There are thousands of ways you can spend and lose your money without generating any measurable business.

As we've said before, there are no shortcuts and no magic tricks. To be successful in SEM, it will take time, effort and money.

How much do I need to spend to generate a return on investment?

This creates major discomfort. Since there is no "standard" pricing, it is extremely hard to gauge how much a service is worth to a business. You might find a trustworthy vendor or individual that knows how to properly spend your money, but they might price themselves out of your budget. Through networking and referrals, you should be able to find people who do great work at affordable prices. A fair price to manage an AdWords campaign is usually somewhere between 20-30% of the campaign budget depending on the complexity of the campaign and the amount of testing you want your agency to do for you.

Remember, SEM *only* works if:

> Number of Clicks
> X   Conversion Rate (likely 2-4%)
> X   Your Average Close Rate for Prospects
> X   The Projected Revenue for a New Client
> -   AdWords Spend (Cost Per Click x # Clicks)
> -   -   Agency/Management Fees
> -   Cost of Goods/Services Sold
>
> =   **A Reasonable Profit**

Otherwise, there's really no point in investing the time or money in this type of initiative.

How long do I need to wait for a return?

This is yet another question that can only be answered with a firm "it depends." This is where most businesses throw up their hands.

Enter Google's Premier SMB Partners[4] (formerly known as Authorized Resellers[5]), big national firms like ReachLocal, Yodle, Dex, and Yext. These are the "brand name" firms in the industry, so business owners are predisposed to trust them as they would any recognizable, national brand. These firms also have large, national sales forces, going door-to-door to tell business owners all the right things:

> *"We'll handle all of your online marketing needs."*

> *"By marketing through us, you can compete with much larger competitors."*

> *"We are successful because we are so good at what we do."*

Mystery solved.

Everyone can stop worrying about marketing online and get back to work. ReachLocal and the rest are here to bring you online success.

Wait a second, are good mysteries ever solved that easily? The short answer is no. Mysteries usually come with different layers and subplots, other stories unfolding, hidden from view and, in time, we get a broader picture of the truth. Buying into the ReachLocal/Yodle (and other AdWords SMB Partners') version of online marketing is like stopping a mystery halfway through because they've already told you the butler did it.

---

[4]blog4biz.co/smbpartners   [5]blog4biz.co/reseller

About Google Premier SMB Partners

You might be wondering what a Premier SMB Partner is. At this writing, this is actually a brand new incarnation of a program that Google has rebooted twice (formerly known as Authorized Resellers). Essentially this is a large agency managing many AdWords clients, and they are certified by Google as meeting their requirements to become an SMB Partner. These firms are required to employ a local direct sales force and manage a large number of AdWords accounts. While Google's public documentation no longer specifies a minimum number of clients, the old Authorized Resellers program required a client base of at least 500 AdWords clients. When agencies become Premier SMB Partners, they are given an unprecedented level of integration with Google's systems, which affords them a dual advantage over any other firm managing AdWords for clients.

Google requires SMB Partners to bring a large client base and employ the necessary human resources and infrastructure to grow, support and bill that client base. However, they do *not* require that their SMB Partners take a hands-on approach to managing their client accounts, nor is there any substantial evidence that Google has stringent ad performance or quality requirements for these firms.

Google provides their Premier SMB Partners fantastic tools and advantages over the small agency because they expect these partners to sell big. However, Google does not demand excellence in *performance*. So while Premier SMB Partners like ReachLocal are widely known for for having a killer direct sales team and the ability to launch campaigns quickly, they are not usually known for superior results.

So what's the secret to ReachLocal's, Yodle's and the others' success? To their credit, it's that locally-based direct sales team. Remember, AdWords is a mystery to small business owners; they don't know where to start, they don't know how it works and they don't know what to expect. The ReachLocal salesperson can answer those questions by presenting the ReachLocal AdWords formula. And with the promise of having campaigns live almost instantaneously, how can the business owner go wrong?

The ReachLocal answer, even if it's not the right answer, makes business owners feel better about AdWords. Human beings are naturally bothered by ambiguity, so we tend to put trust and faith in the person who comes to us with answers, even if those answers aren't the right ones.

The Problem with Partners

There are a lot of issues in the way that firms like ReachLocal and Yodle manage campaigns. Here are some of the key problems:

Unknown Keywords: Google will expand automatically on whichever keywords you provide your AdWords campaign managers, even if those expansions result in completely irrelevant searches. For example, consider the difference between the keywords "basketball league" and "fantasy basketball league." With SMB Partners using proprietary tools, the client often has no way of finding out which keywords are being used to generate traffic to their websites. The result? Clients pay out more money than they normally would for low quality site traffic that will result in fewer conversions.

No Campaign Creation: Using Google AdWords without a real campaign (i.e., an exclusive offer/value/freebie/discount) is a risky bet. Ninety-seven percent of Google search users click on the organic search results, so if we want to convince that individual to abandon the organic search results in favor of advertising, it helps to have a really great incentive. Firms like ReachLocal usually don't tell clients this. Instead, they tend to create generic ads and link them directly into the client's home page or blog page. These destinations are completely irrelevant to the individual who performed the search, because they were looking for something specific. A once-potential client will leave your site immediately and never click an ad again because they feel tricked or confused. Best case scenario? You waste money on poor quality site traffic. Worst case scenario? You harm your brand because you've inadvertently wasted someone's valuable time.

Why then would your agency *not* encourage you to create a special campaign for your AdWords initiative? Because that impairs the firm's ability to launch a campaign immediately (and therefore begin billing you immediately). Marketing campaigns and offers require thought, deliberation, testing, the creation of special copy and special landing pages, all of which cost your AdWords firm time and resources.

Poor Control Over Cost Per Click (CPC): Since firms like ReachLocal are concentrating on generating traffic, not leads, they need to get your ad at the top of search results. Your ad's placement in search results is a product of quality score[6] (x) bid rate, i.e., how much you are willing to pay per click. Because ReachLocal clients (and the clients of many other SMB Partners) aren't creating targeted campaigns, their ads tend to have a low quality score. So to compensate, you have to raise the bid rate. Think about it; a poorly structured AdWords campaign actually costs you *more* money per click than a carefully engineered campaign. Over time, the goal of an agency managing an AdWords campaign is to boost an ad's quality score, so the client pays less per click without sacrificing their position at the top of the paid search results, i.e., getting better results with less money.

Automation: A lot of these firms depend on a high volume of incoming new clients since the average client doesn't last very long. Some people might refer to this as a "churn and burn" approach to business. To be profitable, they need to get their clients spending money quickly with the lowest amount of manual labor possible. The less manual labor, the higher their profits. While these traits are fantastic for the sustainability and growth of companies like ReachLocal, it leaves their customers in a bind.

Google automates as much as possible for advertisers. It is a simple and elegant system that is ready to use by any competent person who knows how to properly manage a campaign. ReachLocal attempts to replace this person with *more* automation. And, even in 2012, software is not an adequate replacement for an AdWords expert creating and managing a campaign.

[6]blog4biz.co/quality

How Have Google's SMB Partners Become So Successful?

1. These big companies have some things they do very well, but making your business successful isn't necessarily one of them. To achieve success, they will:

2. Easily and quickly set up an AdWords campaign to increase your site traffic, regardless of the quality of traffic they bring in.

3. Assure you that you are doing online marketing, so everything is going to be OK. Going through the motions, however, doesn't always lead to success.

4. Take your money at any budget you are comfortable with spending (or losing), even though you need to spend beyond a certain point to receive meaningful ROI.

5. Guard their own reputation online so you can't easily find negative reviews.

6. Do a *great* job on the sales side. Unfortunately, though, the salespeople have no vested interest in your success. They work on commission and will merely try their best to make you comfortable.

7. Automate your campaign with algorithms, regressive analysis, reverse proxies and many other technical things that make them sound advanced but really just reduce manual labor.

So Why Bother with a Middle Man?

You don't have to. You are free to experiment with AdWords
on your own or with the help of an SEM expert. When a small
business client is buying AdWords management, they are buying
two things: experience and trust. We trust the person is going
to tell us the truth on budgeting and put in the time required
to make a campaign successful. Experience ensures that the
person investing time and energy in making your campaign
successful is also skilled enough to do so properly.
That's it. There aren't any shortcuts, unfair advantages or extras
to help you. Reverse proxies, dial tones and SMB Partners are
unnecessary for search engine marketing. ReachLocal may make
it easy to start a campaign, but it will further complicate your
ability to solve the mystery of how to successfully market your
business online. You don't need ReachLocal; you just need the
right person who speaks honestly and does good work.
Putting the SMB Partners in Perspective

I don't want anyone to read this chapter and think that I have
some sort of vendetta against ReachLocal, Yodle and the other
AdWords Premier SMB Partners. In fact, not all SMB Partners are
bad; there are over 30 of them here in the U.S, and not all follow
the model I've tried to expose here.

And yes, I do own a small online marketing agency, and I
freely admit that we are often frustrated by companies like
ReachLocal. Because of the size of their client roster and the
formidable span of their sales force, they are allowed to play by
a slightly different rulebook. Regardless, the criticism that I have
offered in this series is real and based entirely in fact.

The fact is that ReachLocal and the rest have the benefit of:

1. Local account reps on the streets in every major market.

2. Relaxed rules and advanced integration with Google.

3. The ability to aggregate mass amounts of data gathered from thousands of clients' campaigns for the benefit of all.

For these reasons, there aren't *any* firms in the world better positioned to deliver incredible results to small businesses than Google's Premier SMB Partners, especially the really big partners like ReachLocal. The problem is that, very often, they don't. Or maybe it would be more accurate to say they *won't.* As we've explained throughout this series, they have the tools to do so.

They won't craft winning campaigns, they won't consult or advise on winning strategy, they won't try to maximize the value of their clients' budgets and they won't work to maximize conversions.

For the most part, they operate like the old-school yellow pages, ineffectually selling the modern day phonebook listing. ReachLocal and others like them are good at helping clients get their business on AdWords quickly and helping them boost web traffic (whether that traffic is helpful or not.)

My advice to small business owners trying to compete on AdWords: Don't give up on AdWords because ReachLocal isn't getting you results. Do some reading, try to understand the media and basic strategy (beyond what your vendor has told you about it) and demand more from your AdWords vendor.

Find a partner that will listen to you, treat you with honesty and work hard to make you money.

Search Engine Optimization: Why Fake it When You Can Have the Real Thing?

If there's one person to trust when it comes to Search Engine Optimization, it's Matt Cutts. Matt runs Google's webspam team and frequently speaks on Google's behalf regarding rankings and Search Engine Optimization. Whenever Matt is interviewed, just about every blogger/reporter is hoping to leave with a juicy optimization tip or two for their articles.

In a nutshell, although he frequently gives specific technical tips, his advice can usually be summed up in four words.

Make your site better.

In other words, make it run faster, make sure it's well-organized, make sure it's easy to use and, most of all, make sure you have awesome content. I'm oversimplifying obviously, but the point is made time and again by Cutts and other white hat Search Engine Optimization experts. The same measures that improve the quality of an experience for a website's human visitors also help it rank better on search engines.

Everyone remembers the scene from *When Harry Met Sally.* Yes, that scene. Meg Ryan demonstrates that it is possible to convincingly "fake it," and the woman at the next table tells the waiter, "I'll have what she's having."

The so-called Search Engine Optimization experts who spam our inboxes and phone lines every day are basically giving us a Meg Ryan sales pitch. They tell us that they can magically transform our site rankings overnight and that Google, the Harry to their Sally, will never know the difference. Convinced, the small business owner looks up and says, "I'll have what you're having."

But what do you think happened when the woman at the deli got her lunch? It goes without saying that her meal was not as, um, *satisfying* as Sally's.

It turns out that what holds true in most aspects of life also holds true for search engines: whenever you fake it, you usually wish you had gotten the real thing instead. You probably know this firsthand if you've ever bought a bootlegged movie, a counterfeit watch or gotten the Meg Ryan sales pitch at home. And you will notice that most traditional Search Engine Optimization firms, especially those who cold call/email you promising big results, will often leave you deeply unsatisfied.

Now, go back and reread what I said about making your site better: make it run faster, make sure it's well-organized and easy to use and, most of all, make sure you have awesome content. That doesn't sound that hard, does it?

It's not. In fact, "faking it" may actually end up costing you more time and money than the real thing. And that's not taking into account the opportunity cost of poor results and the potentially negative impact of hiring a zealous search engine marketer who over optimizes your site and actually gets you penalized.

The right hosting company combined with a good developer can make your site run blazingly fast. If your site is built in a content management system like WordPress, you should be able to easily solve any organization or navigation issues. Maintaining a weekly blog will help you in the awesome content category.

And just like that, you can get the "real thing": meaningful Search Engine Optimization without the Meg Ryan imitation.

AUTHOR'S NOTE: The section in this chapter on SMB Partners has been updated from a series of posts originally published on my company's blog[7] in September, 2011. Greg Bond, who manages AdWords campaigns for our firm's clients, and I wrote and researched the original series and we received a lot of positive response.

To be clear, I didn't mean to single out ReachLocal. My intent was to talk generally about a particular sales and account management model that is very common within Google's SMB Partner program. ReachLocal just happens to be by far the most visible of these vendors.

I also don't wish to come across as being overly critical of Google's Premier SMB Partner program or the old Authorized Reseller program. Even if they haven't gotten it quite right this time, Google has a long history of meticulously curating its services and doing its best to exert a positive influence on surrounding communities.

[7]blog4biz.co/blog

Notably, Google rebooted the program in 2010[8] to prevent Authorized Resellers from selling AdWords at exorbitant markups. There were also persistent rumors for about two years that Google wanted to shut the program down altogether before finally rebooting it again in the spring of 2012. The vision from Google's perspective seems clear: leverage a local, direct sales force to help put their AdWords product into the hands of more clients. There isn't anything wrong with that, and it obviously represents a natural progression for Google in selling their biggest and most profitable product.

After the last post in our original series on this topic was published, I received a comment from an SEO professional who wished to be identified only as Mark. He wrote:

This was a really fabulous post and really explained the advantages or disadvantages of dealing with companies like Reach Local and Yodle. I know all too well about these companies manner of dealing with them as I used to work for one of them. Good people doesn't always mean good ROI or value for the small business owner. Thanks for taking the time to put this together and for having the nerve to do so. I will redistribute this through my resources.

[8]blog4biz.co/resellerreboot

We followed up with Mark. His credentials checked out; he did indeed work for a prominent AdWords Reseller, and he confirmed much of what we wrote.

We attempted to find other former employees of these firms who might be willing to talk in more detail but did not have any luck.

TAKE ACTION: How To Get More Business Based on the Advice in this Chapter

1. Stay away from "too good to be true" offers, cold calls/emails, MLMs and just about anyone that doesn't come highly recommended by someone you know. And remember, if your site can't be found on Google, how in the world did *they* find you?

2. In AdWords, remember that the Cost Per Click (CPC) you pay is a combination of what you bid for the term and your quality score. That means that the better your ad, the better your landing page and the better your performance, the *less* you pay for your clicks.

3. Avoid ReachLocal and other programs that replace human attention with automated software; this is ultimately bad for your campaign and, quite possibly, your reputation.

4. Don't fall for the Meg Ryan sales pitch; why "fake it" when real success is so attainable?

A SIMPLE APPROACH TO ONLINE LEAD GENERATION

Online lead generation is a lot like the produce department at your local grocery store. We all search for the ideal fruit or vegetable, but superficial flaws don't normally relate to the overall quality of the fruit. As a result, farmers compost millions of pounds of perfectly good food every year just because it's unattractive. Similarly, no matter how good our value proposition is, we all still need to *look* valuable if we want to convert online visitors into leads and opportunities.

We've heard the phrase "don't judge a book by it's cover" since we were kids, but what if we don't have time to read every book to check its quality? Luckily, when it comes to setting up your website and campaigns in a way likely to result in successful lead generation, the only book you need is this one.

Four Ingredients for Successful Online Lead Generation

Own Your Web Property and Use WordPress

As I discussed in Chapter 2, many creative companies and digital agencies host the websites that they build for you. Since they host your website on their servers, you don't have full control. Bottom line? If you want to do any kind of serious lead generation, make sure you have full control.

Why WordPress? We covered this in the Practice Safe Site chapter as well, but WordPress is easily built on and easily maintained, even by novices. A site that is fluid and frequently updated is a site that generates quality leads over an extended period of time.

I also highly recommend the Gravity Forms plugin for WordPress.[1] It's the best contact form software I've used and has a lot of useful built-in integrations. Plus at only $99, it's a very affordable package.

User Friendly Design

Everyone has an opinion when it comes to website design.

[1] blog4biz.co/gf

Before you let all of your individual biases into the equation, take a step back. Ask yourself, "Self, what is the purpose of this site?" It's OK to have a few, but prioritize them. List them in order of importance and focus on those goals throughout the entire design process. And when I say "order of importance," I mean it (no "ties"). Each goal should have a unique place in your hierarchy.

Then ask yourself, "Self, what should the navigation look like?" Navigation is the primary options/sections of the website, typically found at the top or left of every page. In this case, clarity is critical to your site's success.

If your navigation has more than six options in the main menu, go back and try again. If you need to add a small "utility navigation" in the upper right hand corner which might typically include items like Home, About and Contact, that's fine. But you can only have one main navigation, and it should not contain a lot of options.

Finally, on a blank piece of paper, create blocks and circles where you think everything should go on the site. Generally, your top level navigation should end up somewhere near the top of the page or on the left. There are some loose guides for color and imagery (don't clutter), but as long as someone can figure out what you are about quickly and navigate easily, your site will function well enough. Start small, launch with the bare minimum of pages/content and build from there. Like a snowball rolling downhill, websites tend to get bigger over time. If your site is nebulous and poorly organized on day one, imagine what it will look like in six months.

That blueprint you sketched on a blank piece of paper? Bring it to your web designer to use as a conversation starter, but leave yourself open for feedback. Share your goals and ideas, and remember that your designer knows more about this than you do and can help guide you get to where you want to be.

Maintenance

Have you noticed that I have four items on this list but only *one* of them discusses design? Most people drain all of their energy and resources into site design when it's really only a small piece of the puzzle. As long as your site is friendly and easy to use, site maintenance will play a much larger role in overall performance.

Let's say you owned a retail location on the busiest street in your town. Can you imagine making that investment but never sweeping, vacuuming or cleaning your shop? What if you never rearranged the merchandise or refreshed your product mix?

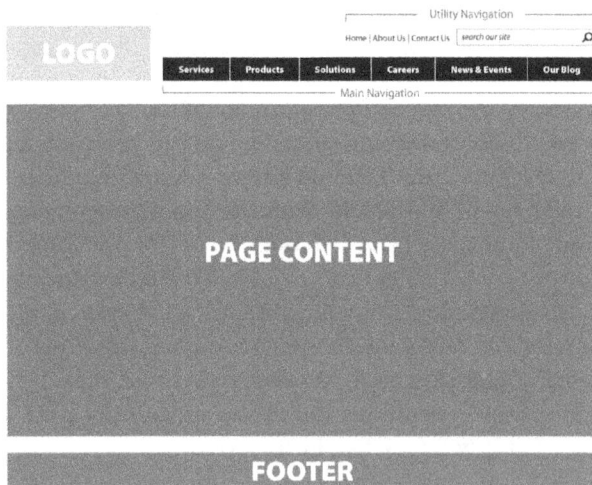

Above is a very basic website layout showing where main navigation and utility navigation would typically appear.

Can you imagine hiring a salesperson to walk the floor but neglecting to train them on your products? Of course not. Retail space is expensive, and if you want to be successful you need to be prepared to welcome your customers, the regulars, referrals and window shoppers alike, *and* meet their needs.

Your website should do the same thing. To accomplish this, you can:

1. Have an online chat operator staff your website to answer questions and help visitors find what they need (we'll discuss chat in more detail later in this chapter).

2. Create blog posts that offer insight into who you are as a person and a business.

3. Take pictures and videos of your work, of happy customers, or just for entertainment purposes.

The possibilities are endless, but the primary goal is to keep updating your site with new stuff. Prioritize your blog and editorial content over pure sales content like product/service pages; sales content is boring and everyone has it. Blog content is friendlier, more personal and, from a traffic perspective, usually outperforms sales content.

If you aren't spending at least one to two hours a week on maintenance, your website will get that stale, old attic smell really quick.

Marketing

This is easily the most neglected piece of the puzzle. If you want to generate leads online, your budget for marketing should be about five times greater than the amount you are willing to spend on design.

Many business owners fall in love with the idea of using social media as their primary marketing vehicle because it's "free." The truth is, you are either going to spend a ton of time or a ton of money trying to generate relevant traffic to your site and, chances are, it will be a mix of both.

The Internet is a crowded place, and Internet users are a tough audience to capture. You are competing with well over a million other people who are vying for your target customers. These are customers who, by the way, are likely spending a much higher percentage of their daily web browsing visiting sites they've been to before rather than exploring new sites. It's not easy building web traffic, so be prepared to put in a lot of effort.

If you have time to invest:

- Dive into social media, go to meetups, speak at events, and network like crazy.

- Optimize your site content for search engines, learn Search Engine Optimization (SEO).

- Create videos on YouTube or Vimeo and post them to your site.

- Repurpose your blogs into an e-newsletter and build a mailing list.

If you have money to invest:

- Create a pay-per-click campaign in AdWords.

- Hire an SEO company.

- Consider offline advertising like sponsorships, but consider how you can leverage them to drive traffic to your site before committing,

Remember that in order to generate leads, you need traffic. Even an extremely successful web initiative might not convert more than 3% of visitors into leads, and big traffic is not likely to appear out of thin air. The Field of Dreams marketing strategy, i.e., "If you build it, they will come" is not in any way viable or realistic.

Getting More Leads from Your AdWords Campaign

Consider the long-standing myth in small business marketing that engaging in an AdWords or Search Engine Marketing (SEM) campaign is sort of like printing your own money. The clicks are cheap, they say; you'll be at the top of the search results, they say; you'll get more leads than you know what to do with, they say.

Unfortunately though, the reality of many SEM campaigns is very different. The clicks aren't that cheap anymore. You will get on the first page of search results if you bid enough for your keywords, but remember that you're competing not only with other advertising results but also the more trustworthy organic results, which account for about 97% of the clicks on any given search engine results page.

You will only have more leads than you know what to do with if you are *very* smart about how you run your campaign. These tips will help:

Focus: Traditional mass media advertising is usually a wasteful endeavor. For example, It's difficult to advertise in a magazine that reaches only your prospective customers. With a magazine ad, you reach out to a wide population hoping to attract the attention of the segment you are looking for and then hope that your message resonates with a significant percentage of that population. AdWords and SEM, however, let us target an audience as finely as we want based on a combination of geography and specific keywords. Be sure to take advantage of the opportunity to be specific. Avoid broad keyword searches that are likely to attract the wrong kinds of people, and be prepared to do some experimentation.

Jump in feet first: I discussed this in earlier chapters, but avoid the trap that comes with trying to "dip your toe in the water" with AdWords, i.e., spending a couple of hundred dollars to see what happens. In most cases, that strategy ends up being a complete waste of whatever test budget the business owner sets. AdWords is a game of numbers and, unless you're terribly lucky, the math just won't work out on a $200 budget. If you're not drawing enough traffic to make a 2-4% conversion rate on your landing/offer page meaningful, your AdWords spending is almost guaranteed to be wasted. If you want to try this, be prepared to go all in for a couple of months at least; it's the only way you'll get any real idea of what your campaign is really capable of.

Use a dedicated landing page: Imagine walking into a car dealership knowing the exact model and color of the vehicle you want to buy. But when you ask to see one, the salesman instead gives you a full tour of the showroom, explaining the features and benefits of all their cars. You'd be annoyed and would probably take your business elsewhere. That's how your visitors will feel if they click on your AdWords link and end up on your homepage.

They are looking for very specific information, and your ad told them that you might be a good fit. Why waste their time? Create a landing page that explains exactly why your business/product/service is a good match for them; it will provide a clear call to action for next steps. We'll talk more about landing pages in the next section.

Support your claim: You know that you offer a great product or service, but most small businesses don't enjoy the kind of brand recognition that big businesses do. There's a reason that most business people know the old saying, "Nobody ever got fired for hiring IBM," but very few have heard "Nobody ever got fired for hiring Jim Bob's Discount Computer Shack."

You only have a limited amount of real estate on your landing page, so don't waste a disproportionate amount of it going on about every little thing that your product does. Focus on why people should buy it and, just as importantly, why they should trust you with their money. Often that means providing meaningful supporting material. Here are some items you might consider incorporating:

1. Customer testimonials
2. A white paper, article or eBook download
3. A video
4. A SlideShare.com presentation
5. Any trust seals that you are allowed to use (i.e., Better Business Bureau, Web of Trust, Authorize.net, etc.)

Consider using online chat to boost conversions:
Often people leave your website or landing page because they never really belonged there. Your product or service just wasn't

a good fit, and that's OK. But sometimes visitors leave for the *wrong* reasons: a minor misunderstanding about what your product does, a feature that isn't explicitly listed, a very specific question that your web copy didn't overtly answer. Often, these visitors won't take the time to call, nor will they fill out your email form and wait for a response.

They may, however, engage in a live online chat with an operator who can help answer their questions. In my experience, it's not uncommon for chat to boost conversion rates by 15-25% or more. We've even seen extreme cases where chat has increased conversions more than 50%. Chat is covered in depth later in this chapter.

Why Landing Pages Matter (and How to Design a Great One)

There's a reason that websites have homepages, and there's a reason those homepages have evolved to look the way they do. Good homepages are designed to provide a formal introduction to your company and help triage the different types of people who might visit your site to the content areas that are most relevant to them. Think of the homepage as your virtual maitre d', greeting visitors, assessing their needs and leading them where they need to go for the appropriate service.

It's exactly the type of experience that we would want to provide someone who is experiencing our business for the first time:

"Good evening, sir/madam! I'm so glad you are dining with us! Do you have a reservation? Would you like a table this evening or shall I lead you to the bar? We also offer service on our patio if you enjoy dining al fresco."

But that song and dance is completely unnecessary for "regulars." In a dining setting, regulars appreciate and expect special treatment. A regular would be understandably irritated walking into their favorite restaurant without being recognized and led to their favorite table.

That's why it's so important that we make our friends feel special on our website. In the age of WordPress and other simple content management platforms, custom web pages or landing pages can be created on the fly. So why not create a landing page and send it to your client or prospect as a follow-up from your meeting or phone call?

A landing page, if you are not familiar with the term, is a page on your website that is designed to stand alone from the rest of your content and speak directly to a particular type of customer or a visitor looking for a specific product or service. Landing pages are often used in campaigns with specific lead generation goals or as a means for providing a specific set of customers/visitors with useful information about a specific topic.

Great uses for landing pages include links from your social media profiles, email blasts or targeted direct mail campaigns. The only url on my business card[2], for example, comes with a scannable QR code[3] that leads to a landing page on my website. This customized page thanks the visitor for following up and provides all of my relevant contact info and credentials.

Landing pages provide a great way to make your visitors feel a little more special and are easily leveraged to increase return on a great many marketing efforts.

Nowhere, though, are landing pages more critical than in an AdWords or SEM campaign.

Wait a minute, you might think. *AdWords is a tool for marketing to strangers, and you just told us that the homepage is for strangers and landing pages are for friends. Why not send AdWords traffic to the homepage?*

Great question.

Your AdWords prospects *are* strangers, but they are strangers who have already told you what they are looking for. In our restaurant example, it would be the equivalent of walking up to the host stand, telling the maitre d' that you'd just like to have a drink at the bar and then getting the whole "Good evening sir" speech anyway. Best case, you'd be aggravated. Worst case, you'd turn around and walk out, and that restaurant loses a paying customer. Using landing pages for these types of visitors is good customer service, plain and simple.

Embracing landing pages, and using them effectively, is a great step towards realizing more return from your website and online marketing activities.

What Great Landing Pages Have In Common

Landing pages are crucial for success in just about any serious online marketing effort. There a few key elements that all high-performance landing pages have in common. They are:

[2]blog4biz.co/erik

[3]blog4biz.co/qr

Targeted: A landing page should only cover one topic/product/service. Your audience arrived at the page because they responded to a specific ad/campaign/offer that they received from you, and your page should support that.

Simple: Don't cram too much info into your page; only give your visitors enough information to get comfortable with the offering and express their interest. Do *not* overwhelm your audience.

To the Point: Good landing pages require a strong and prominent call to action. In other words, what do you want visitors to do after they visit your landing page? Call you? Email you? Download a white paper or eBook? Join your email newsletter? This needs to be obvious and there should be only *one* specific call to action on your page.

Credible: As a customer, you run a risk contacting a company you're considering for their products or services. I can come to your landing page, fill out the form and end up having my time completely wasted. The slightest hint that your firm might not be a good fit for the customer may end up costing you a lead. It's a tough reality.

Make sure that your landing page makes your firm/service appear credible. Try leveraging customer testimonials and trust seals to improve your chances of a successful lead conversion. This is also a great place to leverage blog posts, articles and white papers about the given topic. Never be ashamed to flaunt your expertise.

Many quality landing pages also share similar layout characteristics. The web analytics firm KissMetrics put together a really excellent infographic to illustrate this point[4]

Building Credibility: How to Get More Good Online Reviews

For many business owners, maintaining good ratings and positive reviews/testimonials on sites like Yelp, Kudzu, Angie's List and/or LinkedIn is a necessary evil of doing business. And it's not difficult to see why these services make business owners uncomfortable; they are hard to influence and impossible to control in any kind of meaningful way.

Here are three easy ways for business owners get more of those great reviews they want:

ASK! Seriously. Why wait around for others to pick up the ball on this? Your customers aren't mind-readers and many would be very happy to take five minutes to pay you a small kindness online. But unless they are dedicated Yelp addicts, your customers probably aren't proactively thinking about how many stars and how much praise you deserve every time they leave your place of business. The next time someone tells you what a great experience they had, ask them to take five minutes and review you online. You'll be surprised how many would be more than happy to help.

4blog4biz.co/landing

Make it easy. Use graphics in your facility to remind customers to review you online. Consider providing links or, even better, QR codes to make it simple for customers to find your page on review sites. You can also easily include links in your email newsletters to make the process completely seamless for customers engaging with you online. If people tell you they don't know how to leave reviews, consider creating a quick step-by-step video explaining the process and reminding them again why online reviews are so important to you.

Never try to game the system. Maybe your customers need a little push, so you decide to offer a gift or discount incentive to people who post positive reviews. That would help, right? This is a bad idea and something that a frequent reviewer will almost certainly call you out on, damaging the credibility of your business and of every positive review you've received. Don't try to buy or manufacture good reviews; it's not likely to work. But when someone does give you a good review, there's nothing wrong with acknowledging it on your Twitter account or Facebook page to thank the individual. This will also serve as a reminder to your other followers/fans that you value this kind of input from customers. If this person is on your mailing list, send them a nice thank you email. But don't go over the top, and don't send gifts.

Why Online Chat is Good for Lead Generation

I've been a big proponent of online chat as a marketing tool for years. But what makes chat a good idea and how does it increase conversion rates?

Before I answer that question, I want to stress that online chat is not a good fit for every website. Chat works best on sites where:

A.) A high percentage of traffic is driven by Google AdWords, search engine optimization (SEO) or other online marketing/advertising media.

B.) There are a wide variety of products/services being featured and visitors may need assistance in finding exactly what they are looking for.

C.) Visitors are likely to have a lot of questions about the particular products/services being offered.

D.) You run an eCommerce site and want to reduce cart abandonment.

If your site meets one or more of these criteria, online chat may help your website convert more visitors into leads or customers. So how and why does it work?

Most websites are like vending machines. Visitors show up anytime they like and browse your wares. The problem is that most products and services are more complex than candy or chips. When visitors come to your web page and aren't sure if you have exactly what they're looking for, they will leave. You only have a few seconds to answer their questions. If a visitor has a question that your web copy does not clearly answer, they will leave.

What if, at the exact moment your potential customer was feeling unsure if you were the right fit for them, you could personally ask them if they needed any help, answer their questions or address their concerns? Now you've moved beyond the vending machine model and are serving web visitors the same way you would over the phone, at a client meeting or in a traditional brick-and-mortar setting.

This is what chat does for websites and why, if done well, a chat program can significantly increase conversion rates. In managing online chat for our clients, my firm has typically seen a 20-25% lift in online leads on a monthly basis. We're engaging with the people on the fence, who may be about to leave for the wrong reasons.

3 tips for a successful online chat program

Coverage is crucial. On the surface, a chat program looks like a lot of work. But the truth is that you're not going to be inundated with requests. We expect that (generally) no more than 5% of site visitors who arrive when your chat operators are online are actually going to engage in chat. This means that you're probably only looking at a relatively small number of chat requests every week. The hard part about chat is making sure that you're there when those potential leads show up. Running a chat program means having continuous coverage 50-60 hours a week or more depending on how many time zones, off hours or weekend hours are relevant to your business. If you're not going to be there every day during business hours and a little bit beyond, you're better off not doing this at all. You're going to miss opportunities and send the wrong message to your prospects.

Be present. Successful chat is an active strategy, not a passive one. That does not mean that you pester your site visitors like a used car salesman, but rather that you make sure that your customers know that you are there. Choose a chat package that will allow you to proactively engage with customers under the right conditions (and likewise leave them alone if those conditions are not met.) Also, make sure that you ask specific questions in your invitations, like "I see you're looking at our deluxe Widgets. Can I answer any questions for you?"

115

Service with a :)! If you're going to staff your chat program internally, be sure to staff it with people who understand how to communicate effectively through short, written communications. If you're not careful, it is very easy to misconstrue the meaning or the sentiment behind these types of communication. Be friendly, be genuine and try to exude friendliness and helpfulness in your chats. Use emoticons where appropriate, remember your pleases and thank yous, and end with a friendly goodbye (but only after making sure that your customer doesn't need any additional help).

Leveraging Chat for Customer Service

Over the last 18 months, I've gained a new appreciation for customer service personnel. That's because since the fall of 2010, my firm has been helping clients launch and manage live online chat programs. Most clients we work with have started chat for the purpose of converting more site visitors into leads or sales, but customer support is an ancillary benefit of just about any chat initiative, even if it is not the primary objective of the program.
If you are looking to offer better customer support through your website, there are a lot of lessons we have learned along the way which have helped us deliver outstanding customer service on our clients' behalf:

First, we need to ensure that the customer understands we're here to help them, and we're not going to take an adversarial tone with them. This is the downfall of a lot of customer service operations in my opinion. Unfortunately, though, live online chat is essentially just an exchange of short instant messages, and it's not always easy to convey kindness and helpfulness without the help of a soothing voice or a friendly smile. It's helpful to exchange pleasantries with customers and make a deliberate effort to be not just polite, but exceedingly so.

Second, we try to be as "real" as possible in communicating with our clients' customers. A lot of companies seem to handle customer service with strict rules and scripts. It seems almost as if they are trying to teach their human resources to act like machines. It makes the service rep's job harder and is almost guaranteed to result in inferior service.

We encourage our people to be natural with customers. It's my belief that maintaining the human element in service is a major key for success.

Third, no matter who handles customer service at your company, remember that the more you arm them with good information and make them feel empowered to help, the better support your customers will get.

How poorly managed online chat can damage your brand

When managed well, online chat is a proven means of boosting web lead generation and delivering outstanding customer service. But some people are giving chat a bad name; a client of mine recently showed me a transcript which served as a striking example.

In this case, an individual she knew had gone to a lawyer's web site and, after spending some time on the site, was greeted with an invitation to join a live chat. She accepted and was connected to someone named Jack who asked how he could help. She made reference to a specific legal question for which she wanted a lawyer's assistance.

Jack then asked a number of very specific, probing questions that made the visitor think for a second that he might actually be a lawyer.

But then came the bait and switch.

After several minutes in this discussion, Jack said that he was going to put the visitor "on hold" and attempt to get some information from "the lawyer." In the entire transcript, Jack never referred to his employer by name; he always said "the lawyer" or "they." This type of language would make anyone suspicious, and it wasn't surprising to see that when Jack returned he had been unable to track down "the lawyer." He offered take a message, saying "they" would be happy to call back at "their" earliest convenience.

This approach is misleading, disingenuous and insults the intelligence of the visitor. It turned out that the attorney had hired a third party firm to manage their online chat, and that firm was employing tactics that would likely only damage their attorney client's online reputation.

It's my belief that chat on a lawyer's website should really be for one purpose only: to schedule appointments. At the point that someone asks a complex legal question, the operator should have said something along the lines of "Sorry, I'm not an attorney so I can't give you that kind of advice, but I can schedule a phone conference or in-person consultation with our lead attorney Bob Smith."

A chat operator can also answer "basic" questions like does your firm handle these types of claims, do you serve my area, what is your billing rate, etc. But at no point should a lay person engaged in chat on a lawyer's site pretend to give legal advice.

The other key ingredient to success is constant feedback and coaching from the client. The lawyer in this case should have been reading his chat transcripts and realizing that the operator was going out of bounds.

We work with our clients and tweak our approach and responses all the time based on their feedback to what's going on. It's a big part of why my firm was so extremely successful with a chat initiative for a local Atlanta charity last year which raised conversion rates almost 70%. Our client would read all the transcripts and say, "OK, next time when someone asks ABC, say this." And we would send the client messages saying, "Someone asked us XYZ, and we said this but it might not have been right. How would you like us to respond next time?"

One of my colleagues and I spent a full hour on the phone with a client recently just to break down two chat transcripts that happened to be loaded with a variety of interesting questions. We wanted feedback on what we should learn from those, how we should adjust our documentation and how we should handle them going forward.

If you want a successful chat program, don't allow your operators to pretend they're attorneys, doctors, bankers, contractors or network administrators. Their only job is to help better shepherd website visitors into good client relationships.

3 Ways to Successfully Outsource to a Managed Live Chat Provider

Hiring a managed live chat provider is one of the easiest ways a business can take advantage of the benefits (like more web leads and better quality leads) of an online chat campaign. But it's another matter to effectively outsource this function to a group of outsiders who know next to nothing about your business.

For all the fantastic results that a well managed live chat solution can help generate, hiring the wrong vendor or mismanaging your vendor can seriously damage your brand. But don't worry; I have three easy ways to successfully collaborate with your managed chat provider.

Set Clear and Realistic Expectations for your Managed Chat Vendor. An outsourced live chat firm is never going to be able to know your products and services as well as you do. The good news is, they don't have to. They are not an online sales rep, but rather an online concierge, making your site visitors feel cared for, helping them find their way around your site, or answering simple questions and then coordinating a follow-up with a real expert. Over time, your chat team will be able to take on more and more as they get more comfortable and learn more about your offerings. But unless your business is purely e-commerce based, expect that your managed live chat provider will be warming up leads for your internal salespeople to close. Given that mindset, think about how you sell and what information your chat team can provide you that will make that job easier. Is your sales team territory-based? Make sure your chat vendor provides a zip code for every lead. Is your service licensed or quoted by the number of users in an organization? Have your chat operators ask that question for you. If managed well, your chat team will deliver better quality leads than any other online initiative.

Maintain a Quality FAQ Document. Sending chat operators to man your website without good information is like sending a soldier into battle without a weapon. They don't stand a chance out there unless you give them the tools they need to do their jobs properly. Spend the time to put together a good Frequently Asked Questions document and don't be afraid to revise it over time. If you're not sure what should be in your FAQ, spend some time talking with clients, friends and family; their insight will be extremely valuable. Some managed live chat vendors will maintain wikis or other collaborative sites where FAQs can be modified over time. If that's not available though, even a Google Doc makes an effective way to share and curate support documentation.

Always Provide Feedback. Any professionally managed chat firm should provide you with transcripts of every chat they handle on your website. Your job is to make sure you read them all as they come and provide actionable feedback. Especially early on, your chat team is going to make mistakes as they learn the ropes. Anticipate this and make sure that you're taking advantage of coaching opportunities as they come. Another useful way to manage feedback is to schedule a conference call a couple of weeks to a month into the service and talk things through over the phone. Not only will you be able to coach your operators, you'll get valuable feedback from them as well.

Managed live chat can be a valuable asset to your online marketing, but only if you are proactive with your vendor and take care to properly educate and manage your operators. In the end, though, you get a more cost-effective chat solution than most small to midsized businesses could run in-house and, hopefully, a steady stream of quality leads from your website.

What Do You Do When You're Not Meeting Your Goals?

Launching a new web business, a new website or a new

marketing campaign is a really exciting experience. But what happens when you feel like you're doing everything you should be but you're not getting the leads you want and need? What do you do? It's never an easy situation.

An online sales process (at a high level) looks a lot like a traditional "sales funnel." A large number of people visit your website but only a small percentage will ever filter down to the bottom, producing a conversion or sale. Generally speaking, most marketers would consider a 1-3% conversion rate on a website successful. That number will likely vary depending on industry, price points, competition and other factors.

If your website is failing to convert visitors, there are two likely culprits: either A) you don't have enough visitors to fill your funnel at the top, or B) not enough are making it through the funnel and converting to a lead or sale.

So what now?

If you fall into camp A, focus on traffic. Invest time/effort/money into initiatives like search engine optimization, blogging, PR, social media and online advertising. Build your traffic to the point that a reasonable conversion rate (something in the ballpark of 1%) will yield you the sales you need.
If you fall into camp B, consider changing your message and your offers, revisiting your pricing strategy or tweaking your design. Consider split testing different landing pages or incorporating an online chat program, and try to find a winning combination.

Have I oversimplified a deeply complex business problem? Maybe. But knowing which side of the funnel to focus on, along with the other factors we've discussed in this chapter and in this book, is definitely the first step to getting your website back on track.

TAKE ACTION: How To Get More Business Based on the Advice in this Chapter

1. Build from your visitors' point of view. Sites that generate lots of leads are generally well organized and well maintained. Business owners who pay thoughtful attention to the needs of their visitors are often handsomely rewarded.

2. Use landing pages in your campaigns; you are much more likely to convert a potential lead who has come for a specific product/service.

3. Cultivate a good reputation online. If your customers are likely to look for you on sites like Yelp or LinkedIn, make sure you maintain positive reviews and don't be afraid to solicit them (politely) from customers/clients.

4. Consider an online chat program. When used strategically, and in the right situation, online chat can increase conversion rates dramatically.

5. Don't slip into panic mode when your campaigns don't work the way you hope. Assess what part of the sales funnel is broken and address it strategically.

CONCLUSION

Douglas Adams, one of my favorite authors, wrote, "The knack of flying is learning how to throw yourself at the ground and miss." It's a nice idea in theory but impossible to execute. It's also commentary on a sad reality; most small businesses fail, and poor marketing is one of the leading causes.

It was not so long ago that sales people walked around with a short stack of trifold brochures neatly tucked inside their jacket pockets and a briefcase full of collateral. But times have changed. Now we have websites, mobile applications, blogs and search engines, all of which have made the traditional sales brochure all but obsolete.

When I make this argument in meetings or at seminars, a few people always object, telling me how important traditional collateral is to their business. So I'll ask them how many sales brochures they've received in the course of the last week or two.

The answer is usually somewhere between 10 and 20 brochures.

Then, I'll ask how many of those 10-20 brochures they have actually read. Their whole facial expression changes.

For those of us who receive scores of other people's marketing materials every month but never read them (which is pretty much all of us), why would we ever assume that the collateral that *we* produce is going to be the exception to the rule? Why would my trifold be more relevant than everyone else's; why would I be the one to fly like Superman while everyone else is falling flat on their faces?

The argument is completely irrational. If you don't read other people's collateral you should assume that no one will read yours. Why waste time and money producing it?

You shouldn't.

Why throw yourself at the ground, hoping to miss, when there are safer, more consistent ways to market your business?

The marketplace has created a backlash against people who "sell."

Think about it; marketing and advertising have become completely ubiquitous in our society and we've all developed a strong immunity to the effects. It's not uncommon to see a public bathroom sponsored by a big corporation. We also find our personal and work spaces constantly being spammed through every possible opening including our mailboxes, phones, email accounts and even our driveways.

Our marketplace is adjusting itself, and people who "sell" in the traditional sense are generally looked upon as cheesy, selfish, spammy or altogether irrelevant. That folder full of high-gloss marketing collateral is likely destined for the circular file your client keeps under their desk.

The strength of a relationship is paramount, sometimes over the strength of the service.

If you are a small business serving just about any industry/ category/marketplace, there is a good chance that you are competing against a fair number of large firms who perform similar (if not identical) functions. These firms will be able to offer deeper resources and a larger scope of service than you do. So why in the world would your customers hire you in the first place? Likely, they connect with you or someone on your team personally; they consider you an expert and trust you to steer them in the right direction. They may also feel that, as a small firm, you will give them more custom attention and the flexibility to tailor your service to meet the needs of their business. If so, they feel this way because you demonstrated that during the sales cycle and *not* because they read it in your brochure.

We see a lot of evidence of this in my firm's small business web and marketing clients. Small businesses are Googled early and often during the sales process. The quality of your printed piece does you no good when your website is the reference point that your customer is most likely to consume (and share). More telling is *what* your prospects are most likely to look at on your website.

My team monitors web analytics for many clients. Except in the cases of an extremely product or e-commerce driven client, the most popular sections of their website are likely to be (in no particular order):

- Blog
- About Us
- Newsroom
- Contact Us

The "marketing" pages of the site, the ones that describe the specific products/services being offered, generally get very little attention by comparison. Because "About Us" and "Contact Us" change very rarely, the logic follows that investing time in writing blogs or news releases will be much more profitable than investing the same time writing a new sell sheet or brochure.

That's one reason this book is called "Blog for Business." Because through blogging, we have the opportunity to create meaningful marketing collateral that our prospects are likely to read.

Imagine that: marketing that actually creates value, not landfill.

But wait, you say, *The main premise of this book is that I can leverage blogging to build revenue, but I don't spend my time reading blogs. Why should I assume that people will read mine?*

The other reason the title of the book references blogging is because its contents were created through blogging. Much of the material in this book originated on my blog and has been adapted, expanded, and edited for use here.

So, for as long as you've been reading this book, you have been reading my blog. And this isn't the only time you've unwittingly read a blog recently, I'll wager. Much of the content you read on reputable news, sports and entertainment websites are blogs, as is much of what you read on Facebook and in many of the ebooks and articles you download.

You read those stories/articles/posts, not because the people who wrote them were trying to sell you something, but because you wanted to be informed.

You can provide the same service for your prospects and customers. Personal experience shows that there is no better way than blogging for a subject matter expert to market their knowledge, all while creating the tools required to build a holistic and functional integrated online marketing plan.

There's an Aristotle quote which says, "We are what we repeatedly do. Excellence, then, is not an act, but a habit."

If I've done my job, this book has helped you gain a better understanding of online marketing and how to build the effective strategies and habits that will make you succeed as a marketer every day, and not just the times you were lucky enough to miss the ground.

Good luck!

REVIEW

Blogging will get you more business when you:

1. Start by providing value to people who are online.

2. Consistently provide that value.

3. Use the things you do online to provide value to people offline too.

4. Start with the foundations that can make all marketing efforts online and offline easier.

...but make sure you understand the basics:

1. Many web projects fail. Take time and effort in seeking the right person or agency and pay them appropriately.

2. Own all the major assets required to keep your website live including domain name, hosting account, and passwords — trusting third parties to manage this for you could cause downtime.

3. Get everything in writing. Understand what is included and what is excluded in your contract.

Blogging will give you better search engine results if you:

1. Provide value to people and avoid schemes that fake it. Attempts to trick Google may have dire consequences.

2. Continuously seek to improve the quality of your site: its performance, its content, its usability.

3. Extend the value of your website by using social media outlets.

4. Try to maximize lead generations with both SEO (organic search) and SEM (paid search/AdWords) in your strategy.

5. Understand that advertising takes either time or money, and usually a mix of both. Success in SEM can be undermined by a small budget. Don't try to dip your toe in the water with a small campaign hoping that it will be an effective sample for a full blown effort.

If you hire someone else to do it:

1. Avoid "too good to be true" offers, cold calls/emails, MLM's and just about anyone that doesn't come highly recommended by someone you know. Remember, if your

site can't be found on Google, how in the world did they find you?

2. Provide value through your ad, landing page, and site performance to get the best results.

3. Avoid ReachLocal and other programs that replace human attention with automated software. Automation can be bad for your campaign and, quite possibly, your reputation.

4. Don't fall for the Meg Ryan sales pitch — why "fake it" when real success is so attainable?

If you understand the basics and hire the right people, your marketing efforts will pay off in many ways:

1. Pay thoughtful attention to the needs of visitors and you will be handsomely rewarded with leads.

2. Create website and landing pages specific to the action you are trying to attain. You are much more likely to convert a potential lead who has come for a specific product/service.

3. Cultivate a good reputation online — if your customers are likely to look for you on sites like Yelp or LinkedIn, make sure you maintain positive reviews. Don't be afraid to solicit them (politely) from customers/clients.

4. When used strategically, and in the right situation, online chat can increase conversion rates dramatically.

5. Instead of writing off all marketing efforts as a failure, with online marketing, you can assess what part of the sales funnel is broken and address it strategically. Everything is trackable.

Erik Wolf is a small business marketing expert and author of two books, including the the award winning **Marketing: Unmasked**. He is also the founder of Zero-G Creative, an online marketing agency serving small (and growing!) business clients exclusively. Erik has been featured in T*he Huffington Post, NewYorkTimes.com* and *Atlanta Business Radio* among other media outlets and has been a speaker at national conferences including South by Southwest (SXSW). Erik lives in Denver, Colorado with his wife and two children.

www.ingramcontent.com/pod-product-compliance
Lightning Source LLC
Chambersburg PA
CBHW071855200326
41519CB00016B/4387